For four very special young readers, who are destined
to change the world: Audrey Bouttier, Annie October
Weinberg, Hannah Devlin, and Alexis Lhotka
– H.G.S.

And for four wonderful readers I am so lucky to have
in my world: Hilma Wolitzer, Devon Lawrence, and
Cathy Binck & Nancy Wolitzer
– M.W.

ONE DAY IN EARLY APRIL

From: Bett Devlin
To: Avery Bloom
Subject: you don't know me

but I'm writing to you anyway. This could go into your SPAM. Maybe you're the kind of person who checks the spam. I don't. I found your email address online. You have a strange name. I never met anyone named Avery. But that made it easier to find you. So thank you for having that name. Also, thank you for going to a school that posts pictures of field trips + uses FirstName.LastName@TheShipfieldSchool. org + gives students their own email. I don't go to that kind of school.

So this is awkward but I'm just going to say it. Your dad + my dad met 3 months ago in Chicago at a "building expo", which was at the downtown Marriott. I'm not going to explain how I know but THEY ARE NOW A COUPLE.

That isn't my business, only it IS my business because my dad wants to send me to a place called CIGI this summer.

I've never heard of CIGI. The website says: Challenge Influence Guide Inspire.

That was cut + pasted. Those words are how they got the name. CIGI is a SUMMER PROGRAMME IN MICHIGAN FOR "INQUISITIVE TWEENS 'N' TEENS AGED 10–15".

You could already be bored reading this email. But guess what? YOU ARE SUPPOSED TO GO TO CIGI, TOO.

I'm not going. It doesn't matter what my dad says. But maybe if you won't go to CIGI either it will stop him from trying to force me to go.

That's what I was writing to you about.

Bett Devlin

From: Avery Bloom
To: Bett Devlin
Subject: Re: you don't know me

I think you are confused and have the wrong person. If my papa was in a relationship with your dad, there is a one hundred per cent chance I would know about it. We're very close, and it's been just the two of us almost my whole life, so we're best friends and he tells me everything.

As for my school, it's helpful to have your own email so you can write to a teacher in the middle of the day to ask about a project. (Ms. Pickering sometimes responds in five minutes!) No one from outside my school community or family has ever found my email address before and written to me. The school might need to upgrade their privacy and security settings. I will post a note online.

About CIGI, my friend Callie Workman's older sister went there last summer. I am signed up for the eight-week session. It's kind of a creative-nerd camp. At CIGI you take classes called Bookin' Around and Exotic Robotic, and you also do archaeology searches for real fossils in Dig This! Plus they have microwave popcorn at night for Shut-eye Cinema, where they show a foreign movie before bed, and everyone talks about it together looking for themes.

The best part is they don't force you to do sports. I am not athletic and also I hate to swim. I have some "excessive worries". (Eating expired foods, getting a disease, etc. But drowning is the biggest one.)

You will never have to go to CIGI. I'm the only one of us going there.

Avery A. Bloom

P.S. I'm twelve and I live in New York City. My papa is an architect. Even though you sent your email to the wrong person, I'm curious: How old are you and where exactly are you writing from?

From: Bett Devlin
To: Avery Bloom
Subject: Re: re: you don't know me

I'm also 12 + I live in California. But I've been to New York City. It was the summer + really hot + CRAZY CROWDED. I felt sorry for the people there, but SUPER SORRY FOR THE ANIMALS.

My dad constructs swimming pools + fountains.

Anything with water. He doesn't design the stuff, he builds it. So your dad is an architect. Usually my dad is FIGHTING with architects.

You said your dad shares everything. Do you SEE your DAD'S TEXT MESSAGES? Every time my dad hears his phone *PING* he smiles, like ha-ha-ha, oh this guy just kills me.

I've been camping. LOTS of times. But I've never been sent to camp. We don't have money for that. My dad wants me to go because of you.

He wants me to be your friend.

No offence, but that's NOT something I'm going to do.

Bett Devlin

From: Avery Bloom
To: Bett Devlin
Subject: Re: re: re: you don't know me

Bett –

How do I know you aren't some kind of hacker from Ukraine (you don't say *The* Ukraine, you just say Ukraine, which makes sense because you wouldn't say *The* France) and this is all a scam to get me to reveal the details of my life so that you can drain my bank account or maybe something worse? It's savings only, just so you know, and it's for college.

I'm going to be very careful in answering your email.

I checked the Google calendar I share with my papa, and he was in Chicago in February at a building expo. But that proves nothing.

My papa is not here this weekend. He's in San Antonio for work. Maybe I shouldn't have said that. But just so you know, I'm not home alone. There is an adult here in the apartment with me. Plus this is a doorman building, and since a famous person lives upstairs (not that famous), they are always very careful with security.

I could text my papa right now and clear this up.

I'm going to do that because I'm not allowed to be communicating online with people I don't know.

You won't hear back from me because you have the wrong person and the wrong dad. Although you did have the right camp. But that's some kind of weird coincidence.

Avery A. Bloom

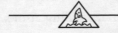

From: Bett Devlin
To: Avery Bloom
Subject: Re: re: re: re: you don't know me

It's NOT a work trip to San Antonio. Your dad's with my dad in Texas. My dad is not LYING to me but he IS STILL LYING. He told me he was going to see his mom. Her name is Betty. I'm named after her but I got rid of the *y* for obvious reasons.

Betty (I call her Gaga) lives in a small town 2 hours from San Antonio.

My DAD IS SO INTO YOUR DAD THAT HE WANTS THE ORIGINAL BETTY TO MEET HIM.

THIS IS SERIOUS!

Bett Devlin

From: Avery Bloom
To: Bett Devlin
Subject: Re: re: re: re: re: you don't know me

I want you to know that I've sent a text to my papa and I haven't heard back.

This is very unusual, but it doesn't mean anything.

I also want to say that when you write in all capital letters it feels like you are yelling at me, and cyberbullying is a very important topic of our time.

And side note: You are lucky to have a grandma, even one who lives two hours from San Antonio (if that's even something real). My family circle is very small. But that's private information.

Avery A. Bloom

From: Bett Devlin
To: Avery Bloom
Subject: Re: re: re: re: re: re: you don't know me

Just to make this equal, here is something private about my family while we WAIT FOR YOUR DAD TO RETURN A TEXT MESSAGE. I had 2 dads. But one died when I was little so I don't remember him. For 11 years it's just been me + my dad. It has to stay that way. We've got everything we need.

My dad's never taken anyone to meet his mom since we lost Phillip.

Did your dad return your text? What's he telling you?

Bett Devlin (not from Ukraine, but from *THE* VENICE, CALIFORNIA)

P.S. Here's hoping we never meet in person.

From: Avery Bloom
To: Bett Devlin
Subject: Re: re: re: re: re: re: re: you don't know me

Bett,

Ignore my last email. Here are the text messages:

ME: Papa, are you in Texas with a man from California visiting a woman named Betty?

No answer to this for two hours and eleven minutes.

ME: Papa, can you call me?
PAPA: Yes. I'll call you in 10 mins.

ME: But you aren't in Texas with a man who builds swimming pools. Right?

PAPA: I'm going to call you. 15 mins.

ME: OK. But do you have a new boyfriend? Yes or no?

He didn't even answer, and he didn't wait fifteen minutes. He called.

They did meet, and they are now in some kind of relationship. I can't believe he hadn't told me, because we never have secrets. He said he was waiting for the right time, and also he wanted to be certain this was something real.

So I guess that's more bad news. It's something real.

Here's an even worse part. They want us to get to know each other and become close like sisters (or maybe even twins because we're the same age?) because it's possible we might become a "family". (I used quote marks around that word because that means I feel ironic about it.)

I told my papa we already were a family. And he said, "Well, I'd like us to be a bigger one."

I would not like us to be a bigger one.

I'm going to tell him I changed my mind about going to CIGI this summer. Maybe I will just stay home and make my own fossils.

Thanks for the heads-up about everything. I hope we never meet, too.

Avery A. Bloom

From: Bett Devlin
To: Avery Bloom
Subject: Re: re: re: re: re: re: re: re: you don't know me

Avery –

While you were talking to your dad I called my dad + said I was in bad pain from an ear infection, which I do get from being in the water since I surf + you're not supposed to be in the bay after it rains because of pollution. But I don't always pay attention to that since the biggest waves are at the same time as the rain because the surf is affected by the storm.

Anyway, I was faking to see if he'd come home early from Texas. He said to take paracetamol + use the eardrops in the bathroom. He didn't even ask to speak with Dee, who is staying here while he's away.

I don't want a bigger family, either. That's WHY I WROTE TO YOU.

I also really don't want a sister or a stepsister or a half sister or a FAKE TWIN or whatever you'd be.

Okay, here's something else IMPORTANT that maybe your dad doesn't know about my dad, but HE HAS A PEANUT ALLERGY. This can be super-dangerous + also it means he can't go for Thai food. Which means your dad CAN NEVER GO FOR THAI FOOD, either. Because even if part of your dad's fork touched a peanut-based sauce, my dad could be in trouble if he was close by because some people spit a little bit when they talk.

Feel free to tell your dad this. A lot of people really love Thai food.

Bett Devlin

From: Avery Bloom
To: Bett Devlin
Subject: Re: re: re: re: re: re: re: re: re: you don't know me

Bett –

I'm feeling sick. I've made mint tea and I'm going to lie down. It's going to be really bad when I try to go to sleep tonight. I have trouble with that anyway. I'm sort of a night owl. I have blackout shades so I can make my bedroom very dark, and I also have a sound machine. I never use any of the water settings, but I can feel calmer by listening to "wind in the pines".

Do you have a sound machine?

I will email you tomorrow after my papa is home.

We shouldn't communicate between now and then for personal health reasons.

Avery A. Bloom

P.S. I want to be a writer, so I notice spelling and grammar in emails and books.

From: Bett Devlin
To: Avery Bloom
Subject: Re: re: re: re: re: re: re: re: re: re: you don't know me

Avery –

I like to read but I don't have time to be a bookworm. Plus I'm not a great speller. I'm okay with that because Snoop Dog + a man named Churchill, who gets credit for the slogan that goes on shopping bags saying: KEEP CALM AND CARRY ON, were both bad spellers. So maybe Churchill first wrote it as KEYP COMM AND CAREY ON. We may never know.

Anyway, spelling happens in some tiny, speck part of the brain + it isn't important in the world now because of spellcheck.

You said NOT to communicate, but I have to tell you one more thing. My dad goes by Marlow but his first name is really DOUGLAS. That's why it's D. Marlow Devlin.

So he changed his first name to his middle name + maybe if your dad thought of him as Doug he might not like him so much.

TELL YOUR DAD.

Bett Devlin

From: Avery Bloom
To: Bett Devlin
Subject: Re: re: re: re: re: re: re: re: re: re: re: you don't know me

Bett –

Just so you know, I am not a mean person, and in fact I was voted Most Thoughtful in my Father-Daughter Book Club because I never forget snacks, but also because I post online summaries of the books for the girls who don't finish the material.

I want to say that your tone is harsh, especially when you write things like TELL YOUR DAD.

My papa came home this afternoon and I did tell him how your dad goes by his middle name.

Do you know what Papa did? He smiled and said, "I'm so glad you two are communicating! That's a great start."

Then it got even worse. He said: "I know his first name is Douglas. I know about the peanut problem, and how much he likes action movies, and that he once broke his ankle skydiving. Honey, I'm crazy about him. I think he's 'the one'."

I mean, no offence to your dad or anything, but *I'm* "the one"!

Avery A. Bloom

From: Bett Devlin
To: Avery Bloom
Subject: Re: re: re: re: re: re: re: re: re: re: re: re: you don't know me

I'm glad you get it now. We have to do EVERYTHING TO STOP THIS. I'm ready on my end. We have a chalkboard in our kitchen + it's to leave messages. I just erased "BUY BIN BAGS" + wrote in really big letters:

I'M NOT GOING TO CIGI THIS SUMMER! YOU CAN'T MAKE ME!

BETT DEVLIN

P.S. I'm "the one" here, too.

From: Avery Bloom
To: Bett Devlin
Subject: Re: re: re: re: re: re: re: re: re: re: re: re: you don't know me

Update.

After dinner my papa said, "Let's go sit on Marshmallow Fluff." Marshmallow Fluff is what we call the leather sofa in our den that is white and looks like a marshmallow. It was an Italian design mistake that my papa made a

14

long time ago, and it couldn't be returned because it was shipped to us from Rome.

Once we were sitting on Fluff, Papa took out a bag that was hidden in a drawer in the coffee table. He handed it to me, all excited.

Inside was a T-shirt. It had a picture of that famous sculpture by the French artist Auguste Rodin called *The Thinker*, the one where the guy is sitting with his hand on his knee. (Though it's the wrong knee, some people say. No one could sit like that for very long. It would be too uncomfortable. You would get a bad cramp.) But this guy on the T-shirt is wearing a pair of sunglasses, and also a baseball cap that says CIGI.

"There are no refunds," Papa said. "Just like when we bought Marshmallow Fluff. You are absolutely, positively going to CIGI. And so is Marlow's kid. We requested that you two be podmates. Marlow is giving Bett her own T-shirt today."

So any minute now (or maybe it already happened), your dad's going to hand over a T-shirt with *The Thinker* in sunglasses.

No offence, but I think we would be really, really bad as podmates.

Avery

From: Bett Devlin

To: Avery Bloom

Subject: Re: re: re: re: re: re: re: re: re: re: re: re: re: re: you don't know me

Avery –

You don't need to throw around "Auguste Rodin". My school has an enrichment programme. My best friends Angel + Summer are BOTH doing it + I see their stuff. It's really not that great.

My dad had a crisis with a bad boulder cracking open at a spa in Huntington Beach, so he left early this morning + I didn't see him. But I was thinking about Camp CIGI so much that I fell off the balance beam in PE, which is my favourite part of the school day. Our unit right now is gymnastics. I'm the best in the class, so falling off is not something that happens. I like gymnastics almost as much as I like skateboarding. Do you skateboard?

So I'm getting a T-shirt??? That's how I'm supposed to know my dad paid for a sleepaway camp named CIGI?

WHAT IS HAPPENING?

A not good thing about having only 1 parent is that I need someone on my side when something big like this takes place. My dad + Phillip (who died) got a woman from Brazil to be a surrogate + carry me inside her for 9 months. So I'm half-Brazilian but I don't have a Brazilian passport, which isn't fair. I never met her, so I can't get her on my side now.

Dad (+ Phillip) used a service + she was paid, so it was a work situation, which is more legal or something. Also, just so you know, D. Marlow Devlin is my biological father (not Phillip). He's African American. So am I. Phillip wasn't African American. I saw your picture so I know you're not African American.

Phillip was from New Mexico, but his parents were from Old Mexico. I don't remember him saying that, but it's one of those things that Dad + I repeat. I'm proud to be a person of colour (POC).

You said you want to be a writer but how do you even know that already?

I know that I don't want to be a dentist or work indoors all day.

Here's something else I know I don't want to do. GO TO CAMP CIGI.

Also – which do you like better, cats or dogs?

Bett Devlin

From: Avery Bloom
To: Bett Devlin
Subject: Re: re: re: re: re: re: re: re: re: re: re: re: re: re: re: you don't know me

We should not be discussing personal things. But I'm not from a surrogate. I don't share my origin story with anyone because there is a cone of privacy around this topic. It's a really big cone.

Dentists are very important in the world and they must be respected.

If you only want to work outside, that eliminates a lot of jobs. But you should know that writers can write outside, too. Like on a patio under an adjustable canvas umbrella. I write outside when my dad and I go away on weekends.

I know there's a difference between ethnicity, race, and culture, but it's confusing. My papa's Caucasian and Jewish, and he did 23andMe, where you send your spit to them and they tell you about your ancestors. My papa found out his ancestors are from Ukraine (not The Ukraine). I don't discuss anything on my mom's side.

I don't have very much experience with animals. I'm actually afraid of dogs. But even though they scare me I have to admit some of them can be very cute. So I like to look at the cute ones, only from far away.

A big dog once jumped up on me in Central Park when

I was very young, and it knocked me to the ground and bit me on the lip. Dr Glossman thinks that this came at an important time in my development.

Avery A. Bloom

From: Bett Devlin
To: Avery Bloom
Subject: Re: re: re: re: re: re: re: re: re: re: re: re: re: re: re: you don't know me

Okay, you should know we have two dogs. Junie + Raisin. We also have a cat, but we share her with the neighbours so it's not fair to say that Prunie is just mine. She also belongs to the Cerronis. She has a collar with both of our telephone numbers but no name tag.

Junie + Raisin are rescue dogs. Raisin came from a "negative environment". We don't know what actually happened, but she growls at a lot of people + 3 different times she tried to bite any man (except my dad) in leather work boots.

Do you or your dad own leather work boots?

I guess they are a trigger for Raisin.

Bett Devlin

From: Avery Bloom
To: Bett Devlin
Subject: Re: re: re: re: re: re: re: re: re: re: re: re: re: re: re: re: re: you don't know me

I don't own leather work boots. Can you send me a picture of your dogs? (If they are cute.) You don't need to send one of your cat.

I won't ever see your dogs in person. Dr Glossman doesn't want me around them (especially large ones) so that really seals off the possibility of us ever living together in California or in our Upper West Side apartment.

Unless of course your dad *gave away* your dogs, which would be incredibly cruel of him, so forget I even said that. You said you skateboard and surf. Does this mean you live at the beach? I think the ocean is beautiful, but also very scary because it's so unpredictable and I'm afraid of drowning.

You're more likely to die in water than in any natural disaster (including all weather-related storm activity).

Most people don't know that fact.

Avery A. Bloom

From: Bett Devlin
To: Avery Bloom
Subject: Re: re: re: re: re: re: re: re: re: re: re: re: re: re: re: re: re:
you don't know me

I go to the beach almost every day. We live 18 blocks from the pier in a small church in Venice, California. Only it's not a church anymore. My dad bought it + everyone thought he would tear it down. But he didn't.

We don't have a garage. My surfboards go out back against the fence.

There are rumors that GHOSTS live here (Is one of your "excessive fears" the spirit world?) since there were a lot of dead people in this place when it was a church. I'm not making that up. They had funerals all the time.

Also, the reason no one wanted the old church was because there is a drug clinic on the same block + people don't want to live by that. What they don't know is that the drug addict people are very nice + they are trying to get help. It's wrong to be afraid of them.

But I don't want to get into anything personal with you because I really don't know you at all.

Here's a picture of Raisin + Junie. They are both amazingly cute. Raisin is the one with all the black spots on her back.

Bett

From: Avery Bloom
To: Bett Devlin
Subject: Re: re: re: re: re: re: re: re: re: re: re: re: re: re: re: re: re: you don't know me

Bett,

Your dogs *are* incredibly cute. Can Junie actually hear through the hole where her ear should be? Assuming that's a hole. It's hard to tell because of the two bandannas.

Avery

From: Bett Devlin
To: Avery Bloom
Subject: Re: re: re: re: re: re: re: re: re: re: re: re: re: re: re: re: re: re: you don't know me

My dog Junie hears fine. Her ear flap is missing from an accident. It might have been a fight. We can't know.

So my dad didn't make a big deal about the camp T-shirt. I just FOUND IT in my drawer yesterday. I cut it into three pieces + put it in our rag box. I told my dad again I'M NOT GOING TO CIGI + YOU CAN'T MAKE ME.

He didn't say anything. But I went online today + his

Expedia account shows he got me a flight to Michigan!

WHAT IS WRONG WITH HIM?!?!? Why isn't he listening to me? He's always always always been a good listener. Then he met your dad + now he can't hear me.

It's like he suddenly built up gobs of earwax. Or else he has really bad swimmer's ear.

Bett

From: Avery Bloom
To: Bett Devlin
Subject: Re: re: re: re: re: re: re: re: re: re: re: re: re: re: re: re: re: re: re: re: you don't know me

Bett,

I think people sometimes go crazy when they're in love. The chemistry in their bodies changes and they do dumb things. Usually this is listening to the same song all the time, or having awkward names for each other. But in this case it means forcing their daughters to go to the same camp and live in a pod together, which really would be a horrible situation that could end in tragedy.

If they somehow make us go to Michigan despite everything we're doing to block this, one suggestion is that you could act like you're falling apart as soon as you get there. In the modern world, *anxiety is increasingly affecting young people.* That was a headline in my school's *Weekly Blast to Parents.* I think it was an inappropriate article because it only made me feel even more anxiety.

If we have to go to camp the plan should be for one of us to leave right away. It would be better if it were you instead of me, because as you know I was actually interested in going to CIGI before all this stuff happened with our dads.

Also, a question: How do two people even have a relationship when they live 3,000 miles apart? Doesn't that mean it's all in their heads?

How do we get it *out* of their heads?

Here is another question, but don't feel like you have to answer: Have you ever had a boyfriend, or a girlfriend if you are gay and know that about yourself already?

I liked Kyle Shapiro last year but it didn't go anywhere. So I don't have any experience in this department.

Avery

From: Bett Devlin
To: Avery Bloom
Subject: Re: re: re: re: re: re: re: re: re: re: re: re: re: re: re: re: re: re: re: re: you don't know me

Last year Zander Barton thought he was my boyfriend + he told everyone, but he was making that up. Holding someone's hand 4 times doesn't mean a relationship.

Neither does keeping someone's hoodie, which was a present. But that sweatshirt is way cool + I'm not giving it back.

I like boys. I've always liked boys. My dad always says he doesn't care who I love as long as I'm happy. Only that was back when he CARED about me being happy.

This kid Robbie Lambert surfs down by the pier + it's weird, because he's in my dreams all the time. He just keeps showing up.

He's 2 years older than me so I don't talk to him. Plus I think he already has a girlfriend but that can't last forever.

Bett

From: Avery Bloom
To: Bett Devlin
Subject: Re: re: re: re: re: re: re: re: re: re: re: re: re: re: re: re: re: re: re: re: re: re: re: you don't know me

Once people know my dad's gay, they assume he's married to another man, and I'm being raised by two dads. I'd like to make a bumper sticker that says: YOU DON'T HAVE TO BE MARRIED TO BE A GAY DAD. Not everyone in this world has to be in twos. It's not Noah's Ark. Single parents do a great job, in my experience.

I've never been to a wedding. Have you been to a wedding? My friend Mia Jablonsky was a flower girl once. But we shouldn't even be thinking about that because a wedding is never going to happen.

We're going to make sure of it.

Avery

From: Bett Devlin
To: Avery Bloom
Subject: Re: re: re: re: re: re: re: re: re: re: re: re: re: re: re: re: re: re: re: re: re: re: re: you don't know me

DO NOT EVEN WRITE THE WORD "WEDDING". Ever. I think it's a trigger for me. Until now I didn't think I had triggers.

Tonight I told my dad I was going on a hunger strike because of camp. Then he drove to Honey Kettle in Culver City to get takeout for our dinner. This is one of my favourite places.

I didn't eat any of the food until much later, when he was out of the room + it was cold. But it was STILL really good. I'm going to need a new plan because the hunger strike thing won't work.

Bett

P.S. If you could be ANY ANIMAL, which one would you choose?

From: Avery Bloom
To: Bett Devlin
Subject: Re: re: re: re: re: re: re: re: re: re: re: re: re: re: re: re: re: re: re: re: re: re: re: you don't know me

Just FYI: At CIGI the kids live in pods of eight girls. There are three pods for girls our age. But maybe we won't even be put together. I'd write "fingers crossed" but it's unnecessary because we aren't going to be mean girls.

If we really do have to go to this camp, we will just never speak to each other, which shouldn't be hard because we don't have anything in common and we don't know each other at all.

I guess if I could be any animal it would be a night owl. (I know that isn't actually a specific kind of owl, but you know what I mean.) I do a lot of reading at night when I'm supposed to be asleep, but that's not the worst thing in the world. Good sleep hygiene is important. That means no screens in bed at night, but books are okay. Also, I wear glasses and for some reason they put glasses on cartoon drawings of owls. (And sometimes they put those graduation caps on them, but that's not what we're talking about.)

Avery

From: Bett Devlin

To: Avery Bloom

Subject: Re: re: re: re: re: re: re: re: re: re: re: re: re: re: re: re: re: re: re: re: re: re: re: re: you don't know me

Night owls are great. I sometimes stay up late, but I don't like having a schedule.

If I could be any animal I'd choose a dogfish. I love dogs + I love to swim. A dogfish is a SHARK. Not everyone knows this.

Also, agreed. No talking IF I HAVE TO GO TO CAMP. Today I asked myself: How is my dad even paying for this CIGI?

Last month I wanted 2 pygmy goats, but my dad said forget it because they are too expensive. The goats were on Craigslist. You can see if the listing is still up (look in LA County – Farm + Garden section), even though you don't qualify to be a goat owner because you need to have a fenced outdoor area. The goats were $250 for the PAIR. That's a great deal! Plus they will ALWAYS STAY SMALL.

But instead of buying an amazing pet, money is being spent on this whole camp thing. It's THOUSANDS OF DOLLARS. Maybe this means I'm not going to college, which should be my choice. I might have to take out huge student loans one day + that would give me a bad start.

Here is more proof that my dad has gone crazy. This old church, which is our house, needs a new roof. It's got bad leaks in the winter, and that means we have to put pots down to catch the water. Junie has bad eyesight so she sometimes walks right into the pots. Now instead of fixing this animal hazard I'm going to camp. Talk about bad priorities.

I could have SO MANY pygmy goats right now. Also, these goats can be trimmed + goat hair is used by knitters. I don't know how to knit but I could sell the hair to people who do.

Bett

From: Avery Bloom
To: Bett Devlin
Subject: Re: re: re: re: re: re: re: re: re: re: re: re: re: re: re: re: re: re: re: re: re: re: re: re: re: re: you don't know me

I also do not knit. But I looked up pygmy goats and they are very interesting. At least to read about. I would do some shark research but I already have enough problems thinking about water hazards.

Today my dad said I have to start "organizing for packing".

That's how he does it when he has to go on a trip. First he makes piles of things he's thinking about taking, and then the piles get sorted until he figures out what he's actually taking. The piles have Post-its on top for better organization. Like "warm clothing", "workout clothing", "formal dining", and "miscellaneous". He read a book called *All in Order: The Norwegian Art of Pile-Packing,* and it was very useful.

I pack this way too because he's taught me that it's the most efficient way.

Question: Does your dad organize first in piles?

Avery

From: Bett Devlin
To: Avery Bloom
Subject: Re: re: re: re: re: re: re: re: re: re: re: re: re: re: re: re: re: re: re: re: re: re: re: re: you don't know me

No. We don't pile pack.
We're last minute people.
Very random: Do you or don't you wear lip gloss?

Bett

From: Avery Bloom
To: Bett Devlin
Subject: Re: re: re: re: re: re: re: re: re: re: re: re: re: re: re: re: re: re: re: re: re: re: re: re: you don't know me

I have a lot of different kinds of lip gloss and ChapStick and lip balms which I keep in a zippered pouch that I bought at a Saturday outdoor market here in New York City, and which has little lips all over it. Most of my lip gloss is medicated because I'm susceptible to lip licker's dermatitis. (I don't know if you've heard of that, but it's a real thing.)

Where do *you* stand on lip gloss?

Avery Bloom

From: Bett Devlin
To: Avery Bloom
Subject: Re: re: re: re: re: re: re: re: re: re: re: re: re: re: re: re: re: re: re: re: re: re: re: re: re: re: re: you don't know me

I'm still figuring out lip gloss.

Another random question: Have you got your period yet? My friends Summer + Angel wanted me to ask you. They don't know you (+ never will) but they are curious.

Bett

From: Avery Bloom

To: Bett Devlin

Subject: Re: re: re: re: re: re: re: re: re: re: re: re: re: re: re: re: re: re: re: re: re: re: re: re: re: re: re: re: re: you don't know me

That's a very personal question. But the answer is yes. I was ten years and eight months old (which is on the young side) when it happened. Even though we had watched a movie (animated) in school about the changing body, I didn't realize that was what was going on. I thought I was dying of a blood disease.

We were in Sagaponack, which is in the Hamptons, and we were about to go to the beach, and I was getting changed (not into a swimsuit because I wasn't going to swim, but into different shorts) when suddenly: blood.

I almost fainted.

People say that and don't mean it, but I have actually fainted before. Three times. What's really going on is that I have a sudden drop in blood pressure and lose consciousness. I've had all the tests necessary to make sure I'm fainting for emotional reasons and not from a brain tumor, like Mr Harrison our (former) mailman.

So I saw the blood and thought I was going to faint, but I didn't. I started to cry (I cry pretty easily, which isn't necessarily a bad thing, because it helps you "unbottle" your emotions). My dad saw me run down the hall. He heard the door slam when I locked myself in the bathroom.

He came over and he was on one side of the door and I was on the other. I sent him a text message: "Papa, I'm bleeding to death."

He said, "Honey, what? Where is there blood?"

I said, "In a privacy zone." Then I added, just to make sure he understood, "Between my legs."

He was really great because right away he figured it out. But we didn't have any "supplies", if you get my meaning.

There is a general store in Sagaponack run by this elderly guy people call Old Gus, who has a big jar of horehound candy for sale on the counter, which children used to eat in the nineteenth century. It tastes like boots. Not that I have eaten boots, but as a future author I can imagine what they would taste like. I stayed home and Dad had to ask Old Gus, "Do you have sanitary napkins?"

The guy didn't hear well and thought he just wanted regular napkins, and gave him those.

By then a line started to form of weekend people wanting to buy things like rosemary crackers & goats' cheese. Dad had to ask again about the sanitary napkins. Old Gus shouted, "Oh, you mean you want pads! *Feminine hygiene pads!*"

Dad said it was awkward. Ever since then, whenever we go to the general store I stay in the car.

Did you get your period yet?

One of my piles of camp stuff is labelled "personal hygiene supplies".

Avery

From: Bett Devlin

To: Avery Bloom

Subject: Re: re: re: re: re: re: re: re: re: re: re: re: re: re: re: re: re: re: re: re: re: re: re: re: re: re: re: re: re: you don't know me

I haven't had my period yet.

The longer it takes to get here the BETTER. I sometimes look at big groups of people + I think: *I wonder how many of the women out there are bleeding.* It's not that great of a thought.

Also, I surf + getting my period means that I'll have more shark risk. You don't read about that in surf magazines. Or maybe you do. I buy the magazines for the cool pictures. I cut a lot of them out for my wall.

My dad said that you + your dad are vegetarians. Me + my dad are big meat-eaters. I LOVE animals, but I eat meat because those animals would not be alive at all WITHOUT A FARM that was raising them to take to market. So you aren't saving an animal by not eating meat. You are keeping one from being born.

If you think about it then it makes more sense, but a lot of people don't do this.

My favourite meat is bacon.

Bett

From: Avery Bloom
To: Bett Devlin
Subject: Re: re: re: re: re: re: re: re: re: re: re: re: re: re: re: re: re: re: re: re: re: re: re: re: re: re: re: re: re: you don't know me

I feel like I should tell you that people who eat bacon have a much greater chance of getting cancer than people who don't, because the nitrates are really bad for you.

Also, bacon can clog your arteries. Not now, but a long time from now, way after you've eaten the bacon and thought it was so delicious.

Avery

From: Bett Devlin
To: Avery Bloom
Subject: Re: re: re: re: re: re: re: re: re: re: re: re: re: re: re: re: re: re: re: re: re: re: re: re: re: re: re: re: re: you don't know me

Don't worry about me eating bacon, because doctors will have figured out how to fix any bacon problem by the time we are old.

Me + Dad go to a clinic when we're sick. I like Dr Nguyen. He once flew Air Force aeroplanes. He has a bowl of fun-size candy bars right on his desk that's for everyone.

I don't know why they try to sell smaller candy bars as being more fun than the bigger ones. That's just a lie.

Bett

From: Avery Bloom
To: Bett Devlin
Subject: Re: re: re: re: re: re: re: re: re: re: re: re: re: re: re: re: re: re: re: re: re: re: re: re: re: re: re: re: re: re: re: re: you don't know me

I leave on Thursday for CIGI. I'm flying by myself. I'm very nervous about the plane. We aren't flying over water, but what if we crash-land? Which would be worse: smashing into the ground or hitting a body of water? The water is also a very hard landing, and if you survive you can then die from drowning. One would probably be instant death, and the other could take a little longer. I'm getting a headache from the choice.

My dad will really regret sending me to camp if either thing happens to me.

I'm all packed. Are you all packed?

Avery

From: Bett Devlin

To: Avery Bloom

Subject: Re: re: re: re: re: re: re: re: re: re: re: re: re: re: re: re: re: re: re: re: re: re: re: re: re: re: re: re: re: re: re: re: re: you don't know me

I haven't even started packing. I know they sent that big list with what to bring but I threw it away. I looked at it really quickly before I put it in the garbage, which was enough to know I wasn't going to bring one "personal attachment item" like a teddy bear, which is the example they gave. Talk about baby time.

My personal attachment item would be one of my dogs + that wouldn't work. Are you bringing something? If some of the girls show up with their old ratty blankets I'm going to just fall over.

All I know that I'm FOR SURE BRINGING is my iPad. (My whole school got them, donated.) It says they "strongly discourage personal technology" (isn't it partly a science + technology camp?) but I told my dad that I'm NOT LEAVING HERE WITHOUT MY iPAD. So I think he is going to ask for a technology waiver.

If you have one, you should bring it. We may need to communicate. But we both agree that we will NOT SPEAK TO EACH OTHER AT CAMP. So not that kind of communicating.

I'll be wearing a skirt + an orange T-shirt in case you

have trouble figuring out who I am. Orange is my favourite colour.

Bett

P.S. I just checked my dad's email account before I pressed send. (He's out of the house.) I have a SUPER-BIG NEWS FLASH! I think you should sit down before you read it, because of your fainting problem:

MY DAD + YOUR DAD ARE GOING TO CHINA TOGETHER WHILE WE ARE AT CAMP!

That's right, CHINA. They will be travelling for 8 WEEKS, IN A FOREIGN COUNTRY + PROBABLY TOTALLY OUT OF REACH IF WE HAVE AN EMERGENCY.

I hope you didn't feel too dizzy reading that.

Bett

From: Avery Bloom
To: Bett Devlin
Subject: Re: re: re: re: re: re: re: re: re: re: re: re: re: re: re: re: re: re: re: re: re: re: re: re: re: re: re: re: re: re: re: re: re: re: re: re: re: re: you don't know me

China? Really?! I'm having trouble breathing, and I just used my inhaler and it's not working. Uncontrolled emotions can constrict the smooth muscles of the lungs and cause chest tightness. It's called *nervous asthma*. It's happened to me before and it's happening to me right now.

I really try not to use my inhaler because you can get dependent on them, and that can lead to a bad situation.

When I get very upset (like right now) I go to one of my books. I'm always reading several at the same time. They are all over the apartment, but with bookmarks to hold my place, not open facedown, because that breaks their spines. This is how much the news has upset me: I can't even concentrate enough to read.

Our fathers are going to China and we're being sent to a sleepaway camp and our lives are spinning out of control.

A

Hello, Avery! Hello, Bett! (In alphabetical order!)

WELCOME TO CAMP! We each hid a copy of this same note in your bags. We have no idea if CIGI is the most awesome programme out there, but we figured it would have enough outdoor stuff for Bett, and enough indoor stuff for Avery.

We want you to get to know each other without us around to interfere, because we think this is the start of a friendship that will last for a long, long time.

As in forever.

So have fun, you guys. Find fossils. Study robotics. Open your hearts. Go in new directions. And in 8 weeks maybe we'll be on our way to having 2 families of 2 become 1 family of 4. Or, as they might put it in the Rockin' the Numbers class at CIGI: $(2x2)=4$ or $(-2)2= (-2) \times (-2) = 4$

We love you so much,

Papa + Dad

From: Bett Devlin
To: Avery Bloom
Subject: Re: re: re: re: re: re: re: re: re: re: re: re: re: re: re: re: re: re: re: re: re: re: re: re: re: re: re: re: re: re: re: re: re: re: re: re: you don't know me

A –

Good thing we both got the technology waiver. Even though we agreed that it makes sense NOT TO TALK TO EACH OTHER AT ALL, there's still stuff to say, now that we're here.

I was thinking you would beat me to CIGI, but Daniel the Camp Director explained that people who come from the farthest away are always earlier than the people who are close by. New York is closer than Los Angeles.

Plus it wasn't your fault there was a thunderstorm + your plane got delayed.

You didn't miss ANYTHING. All that happened was hearing boring rules (I didn't listen because it was the same stuff that was in the packet + who would bring a knife or fireworks to camp?).

I unpacked + found the dad note. I got so mad at the words, "As in forever".

Whenever I complain about something, my dad always says "Bett, nothing lasts forever," so that line came from your dad, not mine. But I really think the WHOLE thing sounded like your dad since my dad DOESN'T EVER WRITE ME LETTERS.

I'm not saying your dad is more into this than mine. I think they are into it the same amount, which is how we got to be here digging up fossils. I bet the camp hides them ahead of time because I saw that on the TV show *Copter Crew: Among the Missing*, where the team took dogs to a landslide area. They had to hide real dead bodies for the three beagles or they'd lose interest. At a place like CIGI they probably go bury a bunch of fossils, because otherwise we'd stop looking.

Anyway, while we're here fake-fossil hunting, THE DADS HAVE THEIR OWN PLAN. They admitted that they were going to China. But I didn't know it was to RIDE MOTORCYCLES. I found that out at the airport.

THIS IS JUST LIKE MY DAD. He gets an idea about stuff + then he just goes + does it. Remind me to write to you about the hot-air balloon ride we were taking in New Mexico when it started snowing.

Did YOU know about the MOTORCYCLES + not tell me? Is your papa a big rider? If he's like you, I sort of doubt it.

My dad can do A LOT of stuff, like drive a forklift + parasail + Jet Ski + snowboard + he once owned a hang glider. For a long time he's said that he wanted to go on a real motorcycle adventure + it was going to be with ME when I'm older. That was OUR PLAN. So this is really wrong.

Write back to me. It looks like I'm sleeping but I'm not because of the time change + because of the motorcycle trip that is happening without me.

Bett

P.S. Tomorrow we pick animals to take care of. I'm going to ask for the PIGS. I heard the WORST choice is the chickens because they don't bond.

From: Avery Bloom
To: Bett Devlin
Subject: Re: re: re: re: re: re: re: re: re: re: re: re: re: re: re: re: re: re: re: re: re: re: re: re: re: re: re: re: re: re: re: re: re: you don't know me

B –

It's 3:02 a.m. You're asleep. I asked our camp counsellor, Rachel, to show me where you are. She pointed to a lump, but your head is completely under the blanket. Naturally,

I was worried that you're going to suffocate. But Rachel whispered, "Oh, Bett Devlin does everything her own way."

So, you've been here for only ten hours and our counsellor already thinks of you as some sort of impressive rebel. That would never happen to me.

I'm trying to sleep but I have travel nerves. Added to that I have Papa's safety to worry about. Motorcycles are dangerous. Everyone knows that. We had a neighbour who was a neurologist! And he was a real talker. Papa is such a hypocrite. Whenever we travel he is all about our personal safety, which probably means that my worries are in my DNA.

Being in love has changed him.

A

P.S. I already decided that I'm going to pick a chicken for my animal, despite what you said. I feel that they are underrated because of having very small brains. I have a plan that maybe I can bulk up my chicken's IQ using parrot-training techniques. I could then write about it for the National Young Writers' Contest, which is in September. I hope to enter in three different categories.

I'll see you tomorrow, but of course I won't talk to you. There are lots of people here, so we'll each make our own friends. If we find ourselves standing around in the same group of people, one of us can just sort of wander off and be interested in plants.

From: Bett Devlin

To: Avery Bloom

Subject: Re: re: re: re: re: re: re: re: re: re: re: re: re: re: re: re: re: re: re: re: re: re: re: re: re: re: re: re: re: re: re: re: re: re: you don't know me

A –

Just so you know, I did not ask to be moved out of Petunia Pod.

They just randomly picked me. What happened is a girl named Stella came today, LATE, because she had a sprained ankle until maybe a day ago. She's cousins with the super-annoying Dyllan. (That's how it's spelled. Two *l*'s. It's all over her luggage.) She cried because they were supposed to be together + instead she got put in Peace Lily Pod.

I don't want to be mean about it, but crying seems like a bad reaction for a 12-year-old who didn't get the pod she wanted. Also, why are the pods named after flowers? I wish they were animals. I guess this means that'll be another T-shirt I can rip up + put into the rag box.

I didn't really unpack so it wasn't hard to move my stuff when I was picked to go. Anyway, now we will see each other ONLY AT GROUP EVENTS since so many things are done in pods. Everyone says people don't make friends with kids not in their group + we aren't talking anyway, so we really wrecked our dads' plan.

We can WRITE TO EACH OTHER ON OUR iPADS, but I think only if we have news to share about our dads.

Don't tell your dad + I won't tell my dad about the pod move. They are on a thousand-hour plane ride to China right now + have probably forgotten about us anyway. I'm not going to write to my dad. This will be a way of punishing him.

I signed up for my afternoon extra-interest sessions. I picked the HIGH ROPES COURSE. Also CAMPCRAFTS (I want to learn how to build a fire without matches), plus ADVENTURE ROCK CHALLENGE + ZIP LINE. What did you put down?

I guess, if you really want to, we could do 1 activity together (but NOT talk during it) since I'm now a Peace Lily and you're a Petunia. I'd drop Campcrafts if necessary, but the only thing I won't do is Puppetry. Why would they even offer that?

I like your sunglasses. Are they prescription? The lenses seem sort of thick.

B

P.S. I think you're making a mistake with a chicken. My new counsellor is named Benita. (She's nicer than Rachel.) She's from Puerto Rico + likes to sing. She says the pigs get to know you after only 1 feeding, that's how smart they are. Also, if you get pigs you go to the kitchen 3 times a day to get buckets with scraps to use for the slop. I'm hoping to make friends with the cooks.

From: Avery Bloom
To: Bett Devlin
Subject: Re: re: re: re: re: re: re: re: re: re: re: re: re: re: re: re: re: re: re: re: re: re: re: re: re: re: re: re: re: re: re: re: re: re: re: re: you don't know me

B –

I picked all indoor activities. They are:

Express Yourself (Write Here, Write Now!)
STEM for All (Girls Only)
Vegan Cooking Basics: Appeteasers and Sustainable Menu Planning
Puppetry (from Masks to Muppets)

I think we should just stick to what we have.

My sunglasses are prescription. Papa bought the frames for me on a trip to Quebec City, in Canada. They are vintage. We were both trying to speak French there, and we had the best time, just us. I was almost ten and had no clue that in two and a half years everything in my life would be so different.

Today in Express Yourself I started a story, which I thought I would let you read. Look at it only if you are interested. If you're not, just delete.

"As in Forever" by Avery A. Bloom

Leighton Z. Swizzler came from a background that had some privilege, which she understood and accepted because it wasn't her fault. She liked to wear colourful, organic-material scarves, which she would knot and tie and tangle in various creative ways. She also collected books, and left them around the apartment as she read them, though never facedown. She untangled the words inside the books' covers and tied all kinds of ideas together in her head.

Leighton's mother was gay, and it was just the two of them living in an apartment with vertical maroon-and-gold striped wallpaper in the hallways on the Upper West Side of Manhattan, a very pleasant neighbourhood for families.

One night, while Leighton was organizing her organic-material scarves, her mother went to a business event and met another woman. There was chemistry between them. The woman had a daughter exactly Leighton's age. Her name was Court Tappler.

Soon Leighton Z. Swizzler's mom and Court Tappler's mom announced they were in love.

The two girls met, but it did not go well. They were like glue and milk, or like snowflakes and granite.

Court Tappler wanted to do things her way, and she could be extremely bossy, but she cared deeply for animals.

Leighton Z. Swizzler was destined to one day be a fine author. Her life showed great promise, even if, to most people, she came across as being very emotional, a worrier, and cautious by nature (traits seen by social scientists as signs of intelligence).

The girls knew they did not like each other, and decided never to speak, but their dads said they had to learn to get along. "Because we are all going to be together a long time," Leighton's dad said. Then he added, "As in forever."

TO BE CONTINUED.

I know it's not great, Bett, but it's a way for me to express myself in Write Here, Write Now!

It's probably good that you're no longer in Petunia Pod. Late last night, my mind started making a whole internal Power-Point of sad thoughts (with sad graphics). I even cried a little in my bed, but Counsellor Rachel didn't come over with the flashlight app on her phone to ask how I was doing. Neither did any of the girls. I guess they were already asleep.

A lot of times crying is better when people can see and hear you do it.

So far no one has any idea that you and I have an outside-of-camp connection.

Avery

From: Avery Bloom
To: Bett Devlin
Subject: Re: re: re: re: re: re: re: re: re: re: re: re: re: re: re: re: re: re: re: re: re: re: re: re: re: re: re: re: re: re: re: re: re: re: re: re: re: re: re: re: re: re: re: you don't know me

B –

Whoops. I looked over the part of my story that I just sent you, and I see that I made what's called a Freudian slip. (Not sure you know – but that's where you say one thing when you really mean another. But in a deeper way you do mean the thing you said.)

So that's what happened when I said that Leighton's and Court's dads were in love. Obviously I meant their moms.

A

From: Bett Devlin
To: Avery Bloom
Subject: Re: re: re: re: re: re: re: re: re: re: re: re: re: re: re: re: re: re: re: re: re: re: re: re: re: re: re: re: re: re: re: re: re: re: re: re: re: re: re: re: re: You don't know me

A –

I know what a Freudian slip is because there is a store that sells underwear with that name. It's in Oregon. Me + Dad drove up to visit Portland + on that trip we went to the sea lion caves on the coast. Have you been to any sea lion caves? They SMELL pretty bad but the sea lions are really great + VERY LARGE.

I'll read your short story if I have free time. No offence.

But right now I have to go be with Wilbur + Minnie. My pigs need me. Our bonding has been amazing + not just because I brought them corned beef. They've been crying when I'm not in the pen. No joke. Loud squealing, trying to call me back. It's super rewarding. Have you heard them?

Bett

From: Avery Bloom
To: Bett Devlin
Subject: Re: re: re: re: re: re: re: re: re: re: re: re: re: re: re: re: re: re: re: re: re: re: re: re: re: re: re: re: re: re: re: re: re: re: re: re: re: re: re: re: re: you don't know me

Okay. No rush on reading it. I've already written two more stories since then. And eighteen poems. But six are haiku. Here's one:

Fathers abandon
To go east on a journey
How will it all end?

AVERY BLOOM, AGE 12
PETUNIA POD

I did hear what sounded like bicycle-brake squeals coming from the barn. Maybe that was your pigs? I'm trying to hand-feed my chicken (I've named her J.K. Rowling, and if I ever meet my hero author after I become an author, too, I will tell her).

The by-hand technique is how you build a relationship with a parrot. So far it's not working with J.K. Rowling (the chicken, not the author). I'm sort of afraid of her pecking my fingers and causing nerve damage (which would be a problem for a writer, because of typing) so I got a gardening glove from the supply shed and I've been putting a stick in it and holding it out.

I think I made a friend (Dilshad Patel) in cooking class. She's a vegetarian like me, only hers didn't start because she was worried about mad cow disease. Which, you probably know, has had outbreaks in recent years.

A

From: Sam Bloom
To: Avery Bloom
Subject: Checking in

My sweetest Avery (who is now a Petunia! Alert-alert-new nickname!):

By now I know you've arrived, settled in, and that your summer is under way. The camp website posts pictures every night and I've tried to spot you in the group shots. My heart lifted just now when I found a photo of you raising your hand in what I think was some kind of writing class. In the past you've had a shy, slow-to-participate temperament, but in this picture you look like you're getting ready to jump out of your chair. You go, girl!

The camp has been pretty insistent that parents create some space for the campers, so I'm not going to write every day. But we got you the personal technology waiver because I'm out of the country. So you can send me messages 10 times a day if you like. We're far apart but also always near. That's the modern world, right?

The trip is just beginning for Marlow and me. What an incredible adventure! I promise to try and keep you posted without being an annoying helicopter dad.

Love you,
Papa

P.S. Any initial thoughts about Bett? You don't have to answer that right away. Take your time getting to know each other. Are you sharing bunk beds? How is it working out? Also, don't worry, anything you say to me about her is private. No sharing with Marlow. Promise.

From: Bett Devlin

To: Avery Bloom

Subject: Re: re: re: re: re: re: re: re: re: re: re: re: re: re: re: re: re: re: re: re: re: re: re: re: re: re: re: re: re: re: re: re: re: re: re: re: re: re: re: re: re: you don't know me

A –

I'm writing this from the Office because I want to explain something to you. They think I'm being punished, but the truth is that being alone in here is actually really cool. You never get to be by yourself at camp.

Okay, so I'm sure everyone in Petunia Pod is talking about what happened to me today at the zip line, which is supposedly some BIG SHOCKING THING.

CIGI's zip-line course goes across part of the lake. What's the point if you can't leap in? I know that's not how YOU feel about water, but people who LIKE swimming would totally get it.

I go in the ocean at home a few times a week + I have 2 different wet suits. I've jumped off high rocks in Utah into deep water holes. My dad was telling me to go up even higher on our last trip. Also, me + Dad once went over a waterfall on the Kern River in a kayak. That was an accident + it's not something we're going to ever forget, that's for sure.

Okay, yes, I DID unhook the zip-line harness. They don't know that I did this BEFORE I EVEN TOOK OFF down the line. I made it look like my harness was "securely fastened", but it wasn't. I don't want Stanton (the one who's already sort of losing his hair at 19) to get in trouble because he's the counsellor who's supposed to check the straps. He did check but then when he wasn't looking I just unfastened the leg clips again. It wasn't that hard then to undo the front.

So now I'm waiting to see Camp Director Daniel. Maybe he'll try to send me home. That would be great as long as I had a way to buy food + if I could get my dogs back from the kennel. I could be home alone for the rest of the summer. But I'm guessing they're not just going to put me on a plane by myself back to California.

I hope I'll be able to see my two pigs again because without Minnie + Wilbur I'd be crazy right now after all the yelling.

I really don't think they should shout at a 12-year-old like that. I'm not sure it's even legal, because we're paying to be here.

From: Bett Devlin
To: Avery Bloom
Subject: Re: re: re: re: re: re: re: re: re: re: re: re: re: re: re: re: re: re: re: re: re: re: re: re: re: re: re: re: re: re: re: re: re: re: re: re: re: re: re: re: re: re: re: re: you don't know me

Avery –

Since I'm here alone with a big computer on the desk, I was able to do some online investigating, which is the reason I'm sending this 2nd email.

I logged into my dad's email. He's telling his friend Henry WHAT'S GOING ON IN CHINA. So I read a LOT about our dads' first few days on the motorcycles.

Please sit down.

They've already had 2 CRASHES. First our dads hit a pothole + smashed into a kerb. Then my dad hit something called a haw cart. Your dad now has a cut on his head + a very bruised elbow. My dad has an almost-broken collarbone. What's that even mean? Maybe it IS broken?

But they are still out there riding!

You would think that I just told you the worst part – but I didn't. MY DAD WAS TAKEN BY YOUR DAD TO THE HOSPITAL.

PEANUT ALLERGY!!!!

Something they ate was cooked in peanut oil, even though YOUR dad had cards printed up in Chinese that explain MY dad's allergy problem. (That was pretty nice of him.)

It's a good thing my dad always carries his EpiPen, because he used it to stab himself in the thigh, which he has done only 7 times in his life. That kept him from dying a terrible peanut-allergy death somewhere in China.

Then your dad threw my dad on the back of his motorcycle + drove him to a hospital.

My dad never feels good after one of these peanut attacks, but just 3 hours later, they got back on the 2 banged-up motorcycles to ride west. They have an escort car, which they paid to lead them.

Only they were behind schedule now, so they kept going after sunset, which was one thing they said they would never do + that's why they lost the escort car. Then they missed the turnoff for the town with the hotel where they were supposed to stay + ended up being forced to sleep on a blanket in a barley field.

They got all kinds of strange bug bites from that + now they feel itchy all the time. Your dad made a joke about how he is never cooking barley for you again. Is that actually something he cooks for you???

Write back because I may be leaving CIGI soon + going to a local foster home. I hope my foster parents have pets.

What else is there to do with me?

Bett

To: Marlow Devlin
From: Daniel Birnbaum
Subject: Your daughter, Bett Devlin

You are out of the country so I'm writing instead of calling. This is not an emergency. But close. Safety is our #1 concern here, and we have strict guidelines to protect our campers. Your daughter Bett has broken several of our most important rules. Today she unhooked her harness while on the zip line. Then she dropped about 20 feet into Lake Spoon. Luckily she was unharmed.

Bett is well-liked here. When there was a housing mix-up, she immediately volunteered to leave Petunia Pod, and was relocated to Peace Lily Pod. She is enthusiastic about our outdoor activities and has even questioned the morning "thought of the day", which I've never had a camper challenge before. In short, she has qualities we aspire to nurture.

But she also has weaknesses. Bett is not great with authority. (As her parent, you have probably been dealing with this.) She insists that she doesn't do well with schedules. The first few days, allowances were made, but she has still not been able to adjust to camp hours.

Young people frequently wrestle with questions of inadequacy and bouts of sadness. Did your daughter try to harm herself today in Lake Spoon? Does she have a hidden concern she has been unwilling to share?

Bett has been sent to see our camp mental health expert. Until we have that report, we are closely monitoring her behaviour. She has been permanently removed from zip line, but also from Campcrafts, as hatchets are used in that class.

Most sincerely,
Daniel Birnbaum
Camp Director CIGI

From: Avery Bloom

To: Bett Devlin

Subject: Re: re: re: re: re: re: re: re: re: re: re: re: re: re: re: re: re: re: re: re: re: re: re: re: re: re: re: re: re: re: re: re: re: re: re: re: re: re: you don't know me

Bett –

I heard what happened at the zip line from that boy Simon from Chicago. He was explaining it all to Amelia and Zoe and Ry, and I was listening in. He said the camp is worried now about "copycat crimes". So the zip line is going to be closed down indefinitely.

I tried to explain to Amelia and Zoe and Ry, after Simon went back to the frozen yogurt dispenser, that you are a surfer and very used to water, and that it wasn't a crime because no one was hurt.

I think a lot of people are sort of impressed by you. But maybe worried at the same time? And definitely mad about the zip line closing down.

I heard Jasmine say to Dilshad and Dyllan, "Stay away from Bett. She's bad news." I thought that was sort of extreme. Then Audrey B. said that they're making you sleep in the infirmary tonight. Is that true? I'm curious – how are the medical facilities here? Would you say they are:

a)   sub-adequate

b)   adequate

c)   good

d)   excellent

Just wondering.
Avery

From: Bett Devlin
To: Avery Bloom
Subject: Re: re: re: re: re: re: re: re: re: re: re: re: re: re: re: re: re: re: re: re: re: re: re: re: re: re: re: re: re: re: re: re: re: re: re: re: re: re: you don't know me

Yeah, I got taken to the infirmary (dork name for a room with shower curtains dividing a bunch of beds bought at IKEA. I have the same bed from IKEA at home so I know). There's really nothing medical about this place at all, sorry. If anything very serious happened to anyone: Good luck, camper.

The kid next to me has a SUPER-BAD POISON SUMAC RASH. We have poison oak in California. He keeps saying this was sumac. What's the difference?

But they've got good Wi-Fi in here + I found a deck of cards. (The 9 of clubs is missing.) I'm going to see if the Sumac Sufferer wants to play blackjack. Thanks for writing to me.

B

From: Avery Bloom
To: Bett Devlin
Subject: Re: re: re: re: re: re: re: re: re: re: re: re: re: re: re: re: re: re: re: re: re: re: re: re: re: re: re: re: re: re: re: re: re: you don't know me

Bett,

We're not talking to each other and we're still not friends, but I'm on your side. This afternoon I asked if I could go to the infirmary to see how you were doing, and Rachel said it wasn't a good idea right now, and that instead I should work on tomorrow's 3-D printing assignment of an innovative cooking utensil. Mine is a slotted spatula for lefties. My papa is a lefty, and so are a lot of people, including Barack Obama and Justin Bieber. The world doesn't go out of its way to accommodate them in the kitchen.

So even though I couldn't visit, I want you to know that at dinner I didn't eat my lemon tofu cheesecake. I wrapped it in a napkin and then went to Peace Lily Pod and got the red sweatshirt that was on your bunk. (Maybe it's the one Zander Barton gave you?) I told Benita I was going to take it to the infirmary. But instead I went to see Minnie and Wilbur. (They were asleep, but they woke up right away when I got to their pen.)

I put on your red hoodie and then I dropped the

dessert in their trough. I'm hoping they smelled you on the sweatshirt and know that I was feeding them for you.

Avery

From: Bett Devlin
To: Avery Bloom
Subject: Re: re: re: re: re: re: re: re: re: re: re: re: re: re: re: re: re: re: re: re: re: re: re: re: re: re: re: re: re: re: re: re: re: re: re: re: re: re: re: re: re: re: re: re: re: re: re: you don't know me

Avery –

THANK YOU so so so much for bringing Minnie + Wilbur their after-dinner treat. I knew they would wonder where I was. That WAS the hoodie from Zander Barton. That's why it's really big.

There's another kid in this infirmary now + she's also going to spend the night. She accidentally poked herself in the eye with a wooden stick in Puppetry. Do you know her? She's from Wisconsin + wears a little silver bell around her neck, which is super-annoying. She's got on an eye patch now so I can't tell how bad her injury is.

They told us to go to sleep about an hour ago. The Sumac Sufferer wants to leave the lights ON + Puppet Patch Kid and I both want the lights OFF, so that's a problem.

I guess I'll wait till the Sumac Sufferer falls asleep + then

I'll just get up + turn off the big bright light in the centre of the ceiling with all the bugs circling like cars trying to find parking near the beach in Venice.

Thanks again for looking out for Wilbur + Minnie.

Xo
Bett

From: Dr Stohl
To: Daniel Birnbaum
cc: Marlow Devlin
Subject: Psychological evaluation of CIGI Camper #49302

CIGI #49302 was seen today for one hour. She appears to be a bright, emotionally well-balanced twelve-year-old female. Young people in this age group are often troubled by issues of self-esteem, but this was not detected.

#49302 explained that she lives in a single-parent home and that her father is the centre of her life. She showed a strong connection to animals and had highly developed personal preferences (including sleep decisions, eating, and activity choices).

#49302 has never been to camp before. She stated that coming here was not her idea, and she wanted to make sure I wrote that down.

Despite that, #49302 admitted enjoying her first eleven days at CIGI. She likes her counsellor, as well as several members of her pod, and she listed a young camper from New York (#49319) as being "a good person, though totally different from me", who "looked out for my pigs after my zip-line problem". Camper #49319 is not one of #49302's podmates, so this shows the ability of #49302 to expand her friendship circle.

When asked if she had broken any other camp rules besides the zip line, #49302 said a kitchen worker named Connie had been giving her corned beef and coconut cookies. The corned beef was fed to the pigs. #49302 conceded she ate the coconut cookies herself.

Conclusion:

#49302 shows no signs of wanting to harm herself or others. She appears to miss her father (within the normal range for a first-time camper). She understands that her behaviour regarding the safety rules is not acceptable.

#49302 was eager to get back to Peace Lily Pod and see her assigned care animals (the previously mentioned pigs) and go horseback riding. She is also very interested in fire building and an upcoming archery tournament.

From: Marlow Devlin
To: Bett Devlin
Subject: You

Hello from "Zhong Guo"! That's what this country is actually called by its citizens. The name translates to "middle kingdom". So the first thing to know is that the Chinese people don't call their country *China*. We were told yesterday that one explanation for where the western name came from was that when Western explorers arrived they decided that a family named Chin looked like they were in charge!

So, Bett, I got an email today from the head of CIGI, Daniel Birnbaum. He probably thought I'd freak out to hear that you jumped into a lake, but of course he never drove a pickup truck that pulled you by a rope on your skateboard. (Don't tell him about that. Also, maybe don't say anything to Avery, either.) But, honey, I can't come back to get you if you get tossed from the place. So please try to stay on the right side of the water.

Betts, I haven't said thank you. I know that this wasn't your idea of how to spend your summer, but sometimes moving out of our comfort zone is how we grow.

What I'm trying to say is that the world is tough and so are you. I trust you to do the right thing (meaning please follow the safety rules!). Also, here we are writing to each other. You and I never do that because we spend so much time together, and text messages don't count. This is all new for us both.

I'm going to make an effort to be in touch whenever I can. So far China is one of the wildest trips I've ever taken. And you know that's saying a lot! I was unprepared for how much history is here and how humbling that is.

Are you and Avery getting along? Are there other kids

there with same-sex parents? Or is that something kids even talk about? Your generation is a lot less judgmental than mine. Hooray for that!

Love you and miss you so much,
DAD

P.S. We ate scallion pancakes with a great dipping sauce yesterday, and all I thought about was how much you'd love them. We're going to have dinner at Mandarette first thing when we're back, and you can get a double order.

From: Bett Devlin
To: Marlow Devlin
Subject: Zip-line misunderstanding

Dad – Dropping into the lake didn't seem like such a big deal when I did it. But now I KNOW it's a big deal. It was kind of a dare because this kid Eric Peabody said HE was going to jump on his turn. Only he didn't. As Gaga would say, "He was all hat + no cattle." I was ALL cattle. HA! Anyway, don't worry. They let me go back to my pod today.

Avery has been really nice about the zip-line thing. I guess you can tell her dad I said that. I got moved, so we're not in the same cabin. (They call them pods but they aren't.)

I'd love a scallion pancake right now. Especially if it meant we were having it together.

Love you + miss you a lot,
Bett

From: Daniel Birnbaum
To: Marlow Devlin
Subject: Follow up regarding Camper #49302 – Bett Devlin

Mr. Devlin,

Bett is now back in Peace Lily Pod and we've put the incident behind us. But you should know that because of what happened our thought for the day was: "Your best teacher is your last mistake".

I do want to share one other thing. A fellow camper came to Bett's defence. She organized all of the girls in Petunia Pod to wear their T-shirts inside out in support of your daughter. This was surprising because no one had ever even seen the two girls talk to each other. Anyway, we were very anxious to put a stop to any "us-versus-them" attitudes at CIGI, so at lunch today we asked *everyone* to wear their shirts inside out for the rest of the day.

We're finding this is breaking down some of the barriers between pods, which is a great outcome.

Needless to say, Bett does have one strike on her record now.

Most sincerely,
Daniel Birnbaum
Camp Director, CIGI

From: Bett Devlin
To: Avery Bloom
Subject: Re: re: re: re: re: re: re: re: re: re: re: re: re: re: re: re: re: re: re: re: re: re: re: re: re: re: re: re: re: re: re: re: re: re: re: re: re: re: re: re: re: re: re: re: re: re: re: you don't know me

A –

I'm back in Peace Lily Pod. I don't have any restrictions so it's like nothing ever happened, except some of the girls are sort of quiet around me now. Maybe they think GETTING IN TROUBLE will rub off on them.

When you + I see each other in the dining hall it's probably okay to say "hi" + I could also bend the no-talking rule just once to tell you about going to see Dr Stohl. She's a counsellor, only the therapy kind, not the sing-a-camp-song kind.

Bett

From: Avery Bloom

To: Bett Devlin

Subject: Re: re: re: re: re: re: re: re: re: re: re: re: re: re: re: re: re: re: re: re: re: re: re: re: re: re: re: re: re: re: re: re: re: re: re: re: re: re: re: re: re: re: re: re: re: re: re: you don't know

Is Dr Stohl the same woman who teaches the workshop *We Can All Learn from Mice in Mazes*? She's giving a community talk on Friday called "Helping Others: When Is It Appropriate Not to Act?" But she doesn't mean theatre acting.

Half of my pod signed up for the Vocabulary Building Now! class tonight. (Too many of the classes have exclamation marks, don't you think?)

I'm not planning on going, because I saw the flash cards and I know most of the words.

AB

From: Bett Devlin

To: Avery Bloom

Subject: Re: re: re: re: re: re: re: re: re: re: re: re: re: re: re: re: re: re: re: re: re: re: re: re: re: re: re: re: re: re: re: re: re: re: re: re: re: re: re: re: re: re: re: re: re: re: re: you don't know me

I'd do the mice maze workshop if they GAVE US A MOUSE. Or let us hang out + feed some. But Benita said it wouldn't be like that.

I'm going to go to the BIRD-WATCHERS FORUM after dinner. Why is it called a forum? I heard they give us cool night-vision binoculars. Only we don't keep them, we have to give them back at the end. I guess we could do that together if you want.

BD

From: Sam Bloom
To: Avery Bloom
Subject: Checking in

My sweetest angel,

This trip has been very hectic. Apologies for being out of touch for a few days. Marlow and I should have done more research (you know how much WE both like doing that, but not everyone is like us). Marlow is really a "fly-by-the-seat-of-his-pants" kind of guy. Which is sometimes great. And sometimes, well, not so great.

It turns out that motorcycles are illegal in many Chinese cities. We hired a company (we had to by law) and we follow two people in a car who are supposed to be escorts. It's our choice to have them go ahead or follow us from behind. But it's not a perfect system because we keep losing each other.

We've had a few incidents, nothing that serious. This is a beautiful country (maybe best seen not from a motorcycle), and we're having a once-in-a-lifetime experience. At least I *hope* some of the things we're doing are once in a lifetime.

Marlow said you helped his daughter when she had some kind of misunderstanding with a swim instructor at the lake? (He hasn't gone into detail.) She sounds so different from you (and not just because he says she loves all water sports).

I'm really looking forward to August 14th, when we are back together! You are in my heart, my love.

Always and forever,
Your Papa

From: Avery Bloom
To: Sam Bloom
Subject: Re: re: Checking in

Dear Papa,

Are you and Marlow having a good time? I can't tell from your letter.

Bett and I have started to hang out a little bit. In the beginning I didn't think she was a very caring person.

But then I watched her with the camp pigs, Wilbur and Minnie, and with the horses (they all swish their tails when she walks into the barn, and they don't do that for anyone else), and I saw that she was different from how I first thought.

Last night we went bird-watching, which was the first time we did an activity together. I wasn't scared, even though it was very dark out. We could hear the owls hooting in the trees, and Bett found a ladder next to the pig stall and we climbed up the back of the barn and went on to the roof. I wasn't sure that was allowed, but she said there was nothing about ladders or roofs in the rules, so it was fine.

Then this amazing thing happened, which was that an owl flew by and landed on top of the barn really close to us! We didn't even need our night-vision glasses. (You know I love owls, and not just because of *Harry Potter*.) The owl had a mouse in its claws and was going to eat it. (We didn't watch that part.) Bett said it was better not to tell anyone what we saw because it would just make the other campers feel left out, since it was a bird-watchers forum.

Take care of yourself, Papa. I miss you, but you are on a dream holiday with your new boyfriend, and I'm at a summer camp in Michigan, and guess what? So far I haven't needed my inhaler even once!

Love you so much,
Avery

From: Bett Devlin
To: Avery Bloom
Subject: Re: re: re: re: re: re: re: re: re: re: re: re: re: re: re: re: re:
re: re: re: re: re: re: re: re: re: re: re: re: re: re: re: re: re: re: re:
re: re: re: re: re: re: re: re: re: re: re: re: re: re you don't know me

You're probably sleeping now. Everyone around me is. That was cool last night when we saw the OWL, wasn't it? That's your animal! I've seen sharks in the water at home, which is not as scary as it sounds.

Who do you think would win in a fight between a big night owl + a dogfish? I think the dogfish, unless the fight was on land.

Solana in the bunk below me snores really bad. She needs to learn to breathe through her nose. They told us lights-out, but even though I am not a night owl like you, I'll never get used to sleeping on demand.

I'm writing to you because I want to know if it made you feel kind of weird tonight at Fire Circle when Camp Director Daniel talked about CIGI being a FAMILY, and then he went on about how we should appreciate our OWN FAMILIES? But all of that was just his way of getting everyone all worked up about FAMILY DAY AT CAMP.

Obviously you and I don't have any FAMILY coming to see us. You said before that your dad didn't hire a surrogate (like my Brazilian situation). So do you know the person who is your biological MOM?

You don't have to answer. But I'm awake if you do, Night Owl.

Dogfish

P.S. Rodrigo in the barn says we can't move in J.K. Rowling to live with Wilbur + Minnie. He says pigs have been known to kill chickens. I really don't think Wilbur and Minnie would EVER DO THIS, but he said it's too much of a risk.

From: Avery Bloom
To: Bett Devlin
Subject: Re: re: re: re: re: re: re: re: re: re: re: re: re: re: re: re: re: re: re: re: re: re: re: re: re: re: re: re: re: re: re: re: re: re: re: re: re: re: re: re: re: re: re: re: re: re: re: re: re: you don't know me

Dogfish –

I shouldn't be awake right now, and neither should you. Too little sleep can cause heart disease, high blood pressure, and type 2 diabetes. You can read about it online. I'm not making it up.

Okay, you asked me a question about my mom, and I'm going to break my cone of privacy about this very personal family information.

My biological mom is named Kristina Allenberry.

She was a friend of my papa's in college. It's a long story.

Night Owl

From: Bett Devlin
To: Avery Bloom
Subject: Re: re: re: re: re: re: re: re: re: re: re: re: re: re: re: re: re:
re: re: re: re: re: re: re: re: re: re: re: re: re: re: re: re: re: re: re:
re: re: re: re: re: re: re: re: re: re: re: re: re: re: re: you don't
know me

WHAT??? NO WAY!

Me + Dad saw 2 plays last year written by someone
named KRISTINA ALLENBERRY! I kept the programme,
which is why I remember her name. I put it up on my wall
because I liked the drawing of the DOG from the play *DOG
IN THE WILDERNESS* (even thought there was no dog in
the play). We also saw *TELL ME WHEN JIMMY COMES
HOME*.

Is that the same person that's your mom? Are you
saying YOUR MOM IS A FAMOUS WRITER?

Answer back right away. Solana is SO LOUD, and the
information about your mom is SO AMAZING that I'll be
awake for HOURS.

From: Avery Bloom
To: Bett Devlin
Subject: Re: re: re: re: re: re: re: re: re: re: re: re: re: re: re: re: re:
re: re: re: re: re: re: re: re: re: re: re: re: re: re: re: re: re: re: re:
re: re: re: re: re: re: re: re: re: re: re: re: re: re: re: re: re: re: you
don't know me

Yes. She's my biological mother.

That's why my name is Avery A. Bloom. The "A" is for
Allenberry. But I don't put Allenberry on anything except
health forms (though I do end up filling out a lot of those).

I can't believe you've seen her plays!

A

From: Bett Devlin
To: Avery Bloom
Subject: Re: re: re: re: re: re: re: re: re: re: re: re: re: re: re: re: re:
re: re: re: re: re: re: re: re: re: re: re: re: re: re: re: re: re: re: re:
re: re: re: re: re: re: re: re: re: re: re: re: re: re: re: re: re: re: you
don't know me

I just can't believe Kristina Allenberry IS YOUR MOM!

From: Avery Bloom

To: Bett Devlin

Subject: Re: re: re: re: re: re: re: re: re: re: re: re: re: re: re: re: re: re: re: re: re: re: re: re: re: re: re: re: re: re: re: re: re: re: re: re: re: re: re: re: re: re: re: re: re: re: re: re: re: re: re: you don't know me

Don't get too excited. I haven't seen her in eight years.

If I couldn't go to Google Images, I wouldn't even know what she looked like. In the last picture I saw, she was giving a drama lecture in Iceland wearing a cape and a top hat. Weird fact: Iceland is green, and Greenland has ice.

I'm glad I told you about Kristina. But I don't really know her because she and my dad don't get along.

From: Bett Devlin

To: Avery Bloom

Subject: Re: re: re: re: re: re: re: re: re: re: re: re: re: re: re: re: re: re: re: re: re: re: re: re: re: re: re: re: re: re: re: re: re: re: re: re: re: re: re: re: re: re: re: re: re: re: re: re: re: re: re: re: re: you don't know me

Night Owl –

That's really messed up that your dad + the famous

writer Kristina Allenberry don't get along.

Did they have a big fight about something? I don't mean to be nosy. I'm just a curious person.

Also, I wish we lived in a time when people wore top hats + capes in real life, and not just to give drama lectures in Iceland.

Dogfish

From: Avery Bloom
To: Bett Devlin
Subject: Re: re: re: re: re: re: re: re: re: re: re: re: re: re: re: re: re: re: re: re: re: re: re: re: re: re: re: re: re: re: re: re: re: re: re: re: re: re: re: re: re: re: re: re: re: re: re: re: re: re: re: re: re: re: re: re: re: re: re: you don't know me

> The big fight is over me.
> I'm not a fan of top hats.
> I still can't believe you and your dad have seen her plays!
> Good night, Bett-tee.

Avery A. Bloom
Also Known As Night Owl

From: Bett Devlin

To: Avery Bloom

Subject: Re: re: re: re: re: re: re: re: re: re: re: re: re: re: re: re: re: re: re: re: re: re: re: re: re: re: re: re: re: re: re: re: re: re: re: re: re: re: re: re: re: re: re: re: re: re: re: re: re: re: re: re: re: re: re: re: re: re: re: you don't know me

Okay. Only one more thing: PLEASE DON'T GO TO SLEEP YET.

My dad cried at the end of *TELL ME WHEN JIMMY COMES HOME*. I have no idea why. I couldn't really understand what the actor was saying. We didn't have good seats + he was a mumbler.

Dogfish

P.S. I haven't heard from Dad in four days. He's not setting a very good example as a parent right now.

From: Avery Bloom

To: Bett Devlin

Subject: Re: re: re: re: re: re: re: re: re: re: re: re: re: re: re: re: re: re: re: re: re: re: re: re: re: re: re: re: re: re: re: re: re: re: re: re: re: re: re: re: re: re: re: re: re: re: re: re: re: re: re: re: re: re: re: re: re: re: re: re: you don't know me

Dogfish –

I saw both of those plays but my dad doesn't know. I bought tickets with my own money and then gave them to Corrie Cole's mom (Mindy Cole, who is an estate agent) and asked if she wanted to go with me. Corrie's in my book club and her mom likes to take me places because Corrie doesn't do well in crowds.

Was Jimmy that guy on the bridge? Or was he the little boy with the balloon? I didn't ask Corrie Cole's mom (Mindy Cole) because it was awkward since she doesn't know that my biological mother (Kristina Allenberry) wrote the play.

Okay, tell me if you hear from your dad. I worry about the dads whenever I remember to worry. But there's a lot less time here for worrying than at home.

Are you doing the phonics listening games at night before you go to sleep?

Night Owl

From: Bett Devlin
To: Avery Bloom
Subject: Re: re: re: re: re: re: re: re: re: re: re: re: re: re: re: re: re: re: re: re: re: re: re: re: re: re: re: re: re: re: re: re: re: re: re: re: re: re: re: re: re: re: re: re: re: re: re: re: re: re: re: you don't know me

No. I don't do any of the listening stuff. It's our choice. EVERYBODY else in Peace Lily Pod does it. While they do it, I catch up on Instagram. There's a puppy I follow named Ron Swanson and also a rescued raccoon named Pumpkin that lives in the Bahamas + thinks he's a dog. I'd start something online with Wilbur + Minnie but once summer's over I couldn't do it, so what's the point?

Maybe I should start listening to the night lessons. I bet that's why everyone here falls asleep so early.

From: Bett Devlin
To: Kristina Allenberry
Subject: Possible Camp CIGI Visit on FAMILY DAY

Kristina Allenberry, hello!

I'm a new friend of AVERY ALLENBERRY BLOOM. You know who that is. I got your email address from your official PLAYWRIGHT website. (I looked it up to see why it's playwright and not playwrite, which is actually better. The English language has a lot of twisted stuff going on.)

Anyway, I don't want to go off topic. I saw online that you're at a big theatre festival right now in a place called Seelocken. CONGRATULATIONS on being the Artist-in-Residence! That looks very fun, especially if you're into theatre, which of course you are.

I was surprised to find out that Seelocken is in MICHIGAN!

Which is an amazing coincidence. Because GUESS WHAT? I'm with YOUR DAUGHTER AVERY ALLENBERRY BLOOM at a place called CIGI (bad name), which is ALSO IN MICHIGAN. It's an hour + 42-minute drive, according to Google Maps.

I saw *DOG IN THE WILDERNESS + TELL ME WHEN JIMMY COMES HOME* last year with my dad. We have season tickets to the Broad Theatre in Santa Monica, but a lot of times we sell the seats because we are both very busy + season tickets can seem like a good idea until you get them + then they can turn into a ball + chain. I heard my grandma Betty (we call her Gaga) say that. She lives in Texas.

Anyway, Dad + I saw both of your plays (because we couldn't sell those seats).

Here is why I'm writing. We have FAMILY DAY at CIGI (the camp that is SO CLOSE to where you are). A lot of people don't have family anywhere near here. As an example, AVERY ALLENBERRY BLOOM'S DAD is in China on a motorcycle trip right now. So is MY DAD. That's the connection. Avery's dad + my dad met in Chicago a while ago + they are a very serious COUPLE now.

We are supposed to form a family when they get back (we don't know when or where) + that's a huge adjustment for all of us. I live in California. Obviously you know they live in New York.

So me + Avery, who have started to hang out together sometimes, are probably going to have 2 dads now, when before we each had only 1. I did have another dad (named Phillip), but he died super long ago so we've adjusted to his being gone, but we will always miss him. Every year on his birthday we light a candle and then we look at the stars because he told my dad that his soul was going to stretch out across the sky.

Anyway, seeing as you're Avery's biological mom, this means that I'm going to be part of YOUR FAMILY now, too. I wouldn't say you're my stepmother because we haven't met each other yet. But that's why it would be great for you to COME TO CIGI ON FAMILY DAY! You should know that they serve lunch + there are vegan options (just warning you: beans), if that applies to you.

I heard this event is kind of sad for the kids here whose families don't come. They try to make them feel better by taking them to a water park, but Avery hates water so that's not going to be great for her.

Here is something else that you should know. CIGI isn't a regular camp where you make yarn bracelets + do clapping songs. This is a place that wants us to exercise our imaginations with maths + turn things like sports into art +

science. I'm not a super book person like Avery is (not sure if you know that about her, but she named her chicken J.K. Rowling) + I'm not doing any of the extra listening nighttime audio assignments, but already I know A LOT of new stuff.

Avery said that you + her dad were friends in college + that there is a ton of water under that bridge.

My dad cried in *TELL ME WHEN JIMMY COMES HOME* when that guy with a beard was on the bridge mumbling.

DO YOU WANT TO COME VISIT US at CIGI this SUNDAY at 11:30 a.m.? There is a theatre performance of *PHANTOM OF THE OPERA* right after breakfast.

You DON'T want to be here for that.

Please let me know if you can make it. Avery would have written to you herself but she's really busy with a lab project involving spores.

Thank you for your time.

Sincerely,
Bett Devlin

From: Ben Vondrak
To: Bett Devlin
Subject: Re: Possible Camp CIGI Visit on Family Day

Hi, Bett,

I am Kristina Allenberry's personal assistant/summer

theatre intern here at Seelocken Theatre Arts Centre. Kristina asked me to write you because she's in rehearsals around the clock for the new play she's workshopping this summer, *HOLDING UP HALF THE SKY*. She wanted me to tell you that she is incredibly touched that you and Avery have invited her to visit your camp. And though I told her there was no way she could go, given her tight rehearsal schedule, she really wants to try. She is amazing that way.

I would have to drive her there, because she does not get behind the wheel of a car. I only got my licence last month (I am nineteen and just finished my freshman year at Oberlin), and I have my parents' car for the summer but I'm not supposed to take it on highways, only back roads.

If we do decide to go on this trip, we will make every effort to be on time. Just please know that "on time" is not Kristina Allenberry's middle name, if you know what I mean. (FYI, that's not a shareable thought.)

Also, will you and Avery be able to go out for dinner with Kristina? And if so, do you have a favourite restaurant in Woolersville, where CIGI is, according to Google Maps? Kristina likes vegetarian Persian cuisine a lot, in case there is such a place in the area.

Sincerely,
Ben Vondrak
Assistant/Theatre Intern to Kristina Allenberry

From: Bett Devlin
To: Ben Vondrak
Subject: Re: re: Possible Camp CIGI Visit on Family Day

Ben!

I'm VERY happy that Kristina IS COMING TO FAMILY DAY! I told the head of camp (+ I asked him to keep it a SECRET) + he was super happy, too. His name is Daniel Birnbaum + he wanted me to let Kristina know that he saw *TELL ME WHEN JIMMY COMES HOME* 4 times in Chicago + he's a BIG fan.

So we'll see you + Kristina THIS SUNDAY. She doesn't have to bring anything. We heard some visitors bring candy + gum + fun surprise stuff (like Sami-Cal's individually wrapped spicy pepperoni sticks), but we're not expecting any of that.

Okay, thank you, Ben. See you guys on Sunday!

Bett Devlin (+ Avery Allenberry Bloom)

P.S. We're not allowed to leave the camp, so we can't go out for dinner anywhere after.

Hey sweet little Betty Jr. – It's your Gaga!

Sorry this is the first envelope that you're opening from me at camp, but I've been so busy (doing a lot of nothing)! I was planning on writing to you every day – a real letter like this mailed with a pretty stamp, which is something you can keep. Nobody saves email unless they print it out, and who does that?

Here's what I wanted to tell you: Be as nice as you can to that girl Avery from New York City. Your daddy said you were putting up a ruckus at the idea of adding a new daddy with his own kid to your family. Well, I DON'T BLAME YOU! But remember this: You can always come live with ME. That's an option, but don't tell your daddy I said that. He'd take it the wrong way. I'm Betty "1" & you're Betty "2" & the Bettys have got to stick together.

I haven't heard even once from your daddy since he left on his big Chinese trip. After he met Sam, it's like the cheese slipped right off his cracker.

Your daddy's never felt the same way about animals that you & I do, but I've always wanted to buy you a pony. You know that, right?

Okay, love you, baby girl. We'll get through this. We always do. Big kiss! BIGGER HUG!

Your Gaga

P.S. I'm probably not supposed to be telling you this, but your daddy was going to ask Sam to MARRY him while they were in China. So maybe they're already engaged by now. THAT'S WHY THEY CAME TO SEE ME before they left. Your daddy wanted my approval. Only what could I say? I don't even know the guy. He seems nice and all, but one weekend's not much time to judge. It's all a shocker. But I guess your daddy can't wait to get down on one knee and pop the question. When they do get married maybe we can both be flower girls. My friend Diamond showed me a video on the YouTube of a lady who was ninety years old and pushing a walker all decorated with white roses, about one mile an hour & she was a flower girl. It went viral. I'm not anywhere near that old! How about you and me get matching dresses when this wedding happens? I think we'll need to get them custom made.

From: Bett Devlin
To: Betty Devlin
Subject: Good to hear from you

Gaga –

I DIDN'T KNOW ANYTHING ABOUT DAD GETTING ENGAGED!
Are you SURE? Did he say he had a RING? If you find out MORE ABOUT THIS let me know. I wonder if I should

tell Avery. She can faint at big news so I guess for now it will be a secret. But I'm not good at keeping secrets. You aren't either!

Your letter is the first real one I got since I've been here. Some kids get a letter a day. It's mostly postcards + the parents write "I LOVE YOU" as the message. That must get old fast. You can use email if you want from now on because I have my iPad here + I know the camp's Internet password, which is really weak: KNOWLEDGE!

Also, don't worry. I'm being nice to Avery. She's got a good heart. I got yelled at on my third day here for diving in a "no diving" area + she was cool when that happened.

Anyway, we're getting along now + I'm even working on a BIG SURPRISE for her on Family Day. I hope she likes it.

Gaga, I don't want to hurt your feelings, but I'm getting too old now for the pony you're always talking about. Maybe we could think about getting a horse. Or a couple of pygmy goats. Or a capybara (they look like pigs but they're the largest rodent in the world – look it up).

Love you,
Betty 2

P.S. Can I tell Summer + Angel the engagement news? We're REQUIRED to send a letter to someone we think "might want to come to CIGI in the future." Summer + Angel wouldn't want to come here, but I could use the letter to tell them about Dad getting married. They love secrets.

From: Sam Bloom
To: Avery Bloom
Subject: Checking in from the road again

Avery –

Every day Marlow and I are learning so much by seeing this amazing country on the other side of the world.

So far, one of the hardest things is just getting used to riding a motorcycle. I guess we should have trained for it. At the end of the day I can barely walk. My arms feel like I've been working a jackhammer, which I guess is close to the truth.

It sounds like you've settled in at CIGI. I love that. Didn't love that you were on a ladder on a barn roof, but I trust you to make good choices. You always have.

Both Marlow and I are sad not to be there for Family Day, but for us every day is Family Day, right?

Love you to the moon.
Papa

From: Avery Bloom
To: Bett Devlin
Subject: Thank you

Dogfish –

I'm so glad you talked to Camp Director Daniel. We shouldn't be punished for not having anyone to visit us on Family Day. I guess a lot of kids don't think the water park trip is punishment, but you know that I have a drowning-in-deep-water phobia, so it was really generous of you to volunteer to stay back with me.

I'm glad we decided it's okay to hang out. But of course that doesn't mean we're friends or sisters or that we're going to agree to anything about the future.

xo
Night Owl

P.S. Are we supposed to do all the activities as if we have parents here? We should have a plan.

From: Bett Devlin
To: Avery Bloom
Subject: Re: Thank you

We'll figure out Family Day tomorrow. I bet the whole thing will SURPRISE us.

Also, we're getting NEW T-SHIRTS + all the family members get 1. Becky Jansen in Poppy Pod designed them. She's great at art. She put a POSSUM on the shirt + it looks real. I love possums because my friend Angel read a book that explained that they're very misunderstood + she told me all about it.

xo
B

Hello, CIGIES!

Here is the schedule for Family Day, along with our song lyrics. While you will be able to have this piece of paper with you in the auditorium, please try to memorize the lyrics. We really want to put our best feet forward.

All of your family members are inspiring and uplifting, with so many leaders in their chosen fields, but we do have several well-known moms and dads showing up this summer who would no doubt love to answer a *well-considered question* from any of you. In particular, you may want to speak with:

Hallie Lee's mom, Wendy Lee, who is the archaeologist whose team dug up *Xerxes in Repose.*

Bentley McGhee's dad, the famed biologist James McGhee, who is on the shortlist for this year's National Institutes of Health "Scientist of the Year" award.

Josie and Carmen Hernandez's aunt, Maria Hernandez, the inventor of the Hernandez Nuclear Cytoscope and Self-Regulating Centrifuge™, who is coming to see both her nieces.

And we have one surprise guest who works in the very highest level of the arts! I'm personally extremely honored to have her with us tomorrow. We look forward to welcoming these visitors and all the other families and friends.

Attention, water park kids: Your bus leaves at 8:00 a.m. sharp. Please remember that your swimsuits cannot have zippers, buttons, belts, rivets, or metal ornaments, as they could damage the slides or catch on something and cause your swimsuit to rip. Also, all sunglasses and regular glasses must be secured with an elastic strap while sliding. We will be passing these out on the bus when we hand over the towels.

Everyone, have a great day!

Director Daniel

CAMP SCHEDULE – Family Day

8:00 a.m.: Parents' staggered arrival to minimize parking issues

9:00 a.m.: Sample class sit-in for parents. Options include: The Genome, Mitochondria, and Chloroplasts, Oh MY!

Molecular Gastronomy: The Chemical Difference, with Chef Molly

10:00 a.m.: Morning snack (gluten-free)

10:30 a.m.: The Stratford-on-CIGI Players present our version of THE PHANTOM OF THE OPERA

12:00 p.m.: All-camp lunch

2:00 p.m.: Community singing opening song: "Always True to CIGI"

(Lyric Sheet)

We are always true to CIGI
No matter where we go from here.
We are always true to CIGI,
Being smart is nothing to fear.

If you have a brain
Do not refrain
From using it to your best.
We are always true to CIGI,
Which is one big learning-fest.

From: Marlow Devlin
To: Bett Devlin
Subject: Some bad luck

Betts –

So here's an update on our trip. First, Sam's leather travel bag (with both our passports and my phone inside!) got jacked yesterday. We can't be 100% sure it was stolen. There's a slight chance one of us accidentally left it at the hotel, but we went back and it wasn't there. Anyway, we'll have to deal with the headache of getting replacement passports before we leave, which we've been told won't be *that* big of a deal.

Also, we're riding together on one motorcycle now because the second one broke down. On top of that, Sam's phone was damaged when it fell out of his pocket during that minor fender bender, so we can sometimes receive calls – not all the time – but we have trouble making them.

To make a long story short, lots of things are complicated right now. Sam's more upset than me (I can see that he's on the verge of freaking out about everything), but so far he's keeping his cool. I've been trying to tell him I'm using this as a great opportunity to break free from technology and live in the moment, and that maybe he should do the same. But he's not really at that place yet.

Anyway, I don't want you to worry. It'll all get figured

out, and the rest of our trip should be amazing.

Have fun at the Family thing! Sorry we're not together for that, Pumpkin.

Love you so much!
Dad (or Baba – that's Dad in Mandarin Chinese!)

From: Kristina Allenberry
To: Sam Bloom
Subject: A summer camp in the woods and the magical thing that happened there . . .

Sam –

I know it's been a very long time since we've communicated. Years. I've respected your rules. But things have changed, Sam. I tried to call you on your mobile in China to explain everything, but I couldn't get through. Which is why I'm writing.

So how can I put this?

A crazy twist of fate has brought Avery to me.

Or, more accurately, me to her.

And as it turns out, you were the person behind that. Or, more accurately, the daughter of the new man in your life was behind it.

As a playwright, I explain best by setting the scene:

Michigan, July, lakeside, afternoon, high humidity,

82 degrees in the shade. I'm here as Summer Artist-in-Residence, when I receive an unusual email. It explains that our daughter, Avery, and your friend's daughter, Bett, are together at a summer camp nearby. There is a thing called Family Day happening. I'm invited.

So what can I do? I rearrange my entire schedule and go.

My assistant, Ben, drives me, though I have no idea yet that he's never made a left turn against opposing traffic. Still, we arrive in one piece. A stunning preteen named Bett Devlin greets us in the parking lot. She blurts out, "Avery has no idea you're coming today, Kristina! I told her I had a *surprise* for her, but that's all I said."

Now, is this even a fair way for me to reunite with my daughter? In the moment, I feel both confused and afraid.

But I follow Bett into a meadow, where another girl waits, wearing an interesting polka-dot blindfold over eyeglasses. Bett removes the blindfold and yells (the girl has lungs), "SURPRISE!"

Avery looks at me.

I look at her.

She's in shock. She is both 12 and 112 all at once. A wise old soul in a new Camp CIGI Family Day T-shirt. I want to wrap my arms around my child and never let go. But fearing I could overwhelm her, I don't move a foot.

Avery then turns to Bett. "Why?" she asks. *"Why would you do this?"*

"Because I thought you two should be together," Bett says. "It's Family Day. And she's your family."

The tension between them is fierce. If this were a play,

the whole audience would feel the betrayal as Avery shouts: "It was private, Bett! I never should've told you! It wasn't your place to invite her to come here!"

"Well, *you* never would, so *I* had to!" Bett shouts back.

"You think you can do anything you want, whenever you want, don't you?" shouts Avery. "But that's not the way the world works!"

Then Bett says the kicker: "Come on – aren't you glad to see her? I mean, she's your MOM!"

At the word "Mom", Avery breaks. Her expression goes wobbly and she begins to cry. I rush over and pull her into my arms, and she's suddenly hugging me back. Both of us are now crying. And then Bett joins in, but doesn't cry. And then we're *all* hugging, and we're all talking like people with a lifetime of stories to tell.

Oh, Sam, she is wonderful. And Bett is an amazing girl, too. We three spend the afternoon taking part in the activities of CIGI Family Day. We make cricket cages. We play Science *Jeopardy!* We view cooking as a lab experiment. We learn a thing or two, but what we really discover is that we love being together.

Finally it's time to say good-bye, only my assistant, Ben, is nowhere to be found. It turns out that his girlfriend called and tried to break up with him over the phone, so he took off in his parents' car!

Apparently there's no Uber in this remote part of Michigan, so I accept a ride to "town" from camp director Daniel. Before I get in his car, I say good-bye to the girls and we vow to all be together again soon. The camp director then drives me to Silf's Crossing. It's several miles away from camp and no more than a store, a diner, and a closed gas station. I'm told that Greyhound stops here only once a day. I know I can call Seelocken and get someone to come pick me up, but it will take a while, and I had given everyone the day off. Suddenly I think: *No, Kristina, this is fate. You haven't had enough time yet with your daughter.*

Sam, you have to understand I was bursting with emotion, overwhelmed from the day, and also I'd been in the sun for hours. I never do well with too much sun.

So I eat dinner at the Silf's Crossing Café, and study Google Maps. Darkness has fallen by the time I make my way back to CIGI on foot. The whole camp is asleep (they have an early-to-bed rule). I easily find both Avery and Bett, and we quietly slip away and walk to the other side of the lake, where we put down horse blankets and lie on our backs under the blue-black sky.

A moon appears. We make wishes on shooting stars. Words beyond words are spoken. It's now really late. We're suddenly so tired. We start to sing, and then, totally accidentally, we all fall asleep. That was never my intention, Sam. But then when we wake up it's already light out, and I say: "Girls, we have to hurry and get back before anyone finds out you're missing."

It almost works.

But just as we reach the clearing in front of the dining hall, someone cries out, *"There they are!"*

A crowd of counsellors appears, all of them carrying flashlights. "Ms. Allenberry – how dare you!" This is Camp

Director Daniel, a mustachioed man with anger even in his eyebrows. When he'd dropped me at the roadside diner the night before, he was full of compliments, but *whoa*, not now. "You took the girls from their pods without permission!" he shouts at me.

"We were just looking at shooting stars, Director Daniel," Bett pipes up.

"It was dark out and I could see animal eyes, but I wasn't even scared," adds Avery.

The girls are led away by the counsellors. I go to the office, where the camp director continues to yell at me. I'm so sorry, Sam. The long and the short of it is that both girls are now permanently expelled from CIGI. And there's more bad news. They have a "no money back" policy. I checked.

So I step in to help. I make a snap decision. I call Seelocken and they agree to send out a production assistant immediately. I return to the girls and say, "Avery, you're coming with me!" Her face lights up in a way that just stops my heart. She's happy, through and through. I then sign the necessary release forms (she *is* my biological daughter, after all) and Avery is ready to get packing.

But Bett starts to cry. She doesn't look like someone who cries often. So I start to cry, too, but that doesn't help. Bett's really letting go. "Well, what am *I* supposed to do?" she says through tears. "I have nowhere to go. My dad's somewhere in China."

I say that she can come with me. The girls are so happy at the idea that they jump up and down and scream. But Director Daniel has other plans.

"No. Absolutely not," he says. "We're calling Bett's grandmother. She's the emergency contact, not you."

Bett is wide-eyed. "What? Gaga hasn't gone anywhere outside Texas in years. She hates to fly."

Director Daniel won't even acknowledge me after that. I try. I really do. But he refuses to release Bett to anyone but her grandmother Betty Devlin (who for some reason is called "Gaga").

So the bottom line is that after a Family Day at CIGI and a night of absolute magic, the girls are forced out.

But I rose to the occasion.

And now I'm taking care of our daughter.

That's really the headline of this story.

KA

From: Bett Devlin
To: Marlow Devlin
Subject: IT WAS NOT MY FAULT

Daddy,

What just happened here is TOTALLY UNFAIR. I know that if you were with me you would agree + take my side. Kristina (Avery's mom) hadn't seen Avery in so long + we all had such a great Family Day together that she wanted to turn it into Family NIGHT, which totally makes sense. So she came back to CIGI after dark + we all snuck out together.

Just so you know, it was one of THE GREATEST NIGHTS OF MY WHOLE LIFE. Avery said the same thing + neither of us is EVER GOING TO FORGET IT. In fact, Kristina wants to write about all of it, so that means that Avery + I are probably going to be in a famous play. I gave her permission to use my REAL name.

Anyway, the trouble started when I guess Benita (my counsellor) had to go to the bathroom at 3:00 a.m. + realized I was gone from the pod. She got FRANTIC, which is what she's paid to do.

Then she found out that Avery wasn't in her pod, either. That started all the counsellors + staff going crazy about kidnapping. But that is ridiculous, Daddy, because we were safe + just totally sound asleep on the other side of the lake, so we didn't hear them calling our names.

A kid named Lana Dewey started saying that she thought she saw SLENDER MAN in the woods. That didn't help.

Anyway, they didn't EVER even find us. We woke up really early + walked back to camp for breakfast. That was when we got kicked out.

What's weird is that I was just getting to like it here + today they were finally going to reopen the zip line.

Right now Gaga is flying up from Texas to get me. So this emergency situation ended her no-flying thing. That's good news – right? You've always said that one day she will just decide to fly again. Well, now we have the day. She's going to rent a car at the airport in Detroit + come straight here.

Avery went to a theatre institute called Seelocken with Kristina.

DAD, here's the thing: I WANT TO GO to Seelocken so bad. That's REALLY WHAT I'M WRITING ABOUT.

If you get this soon, DO YOU THINK YOU COULD CALL DIRECTOR DANIEL + say I can go to SEELOCKEN instead of with Gaga (no offence)? You know I love her so much, but Texas in the summer is a million degrees + I really want to be with Avery. Plus, Kristina is an amazing person + she said it would be great to have me learn theatre stuff because it's useful in life.

Write back RIGHT AWAY. Gaga could drive me + get me settled in + then fly back to Texas. That's a really great plan I think.

I hope China is super fun + that SPECIAL THINGS are going on with you + Sam in your relationship, which I'm sure you'll both tell us about when you're ready.

Love,
Bett

P.S. It was true when you said that the experience of CIGI would make my life bigger. It feels SO BIG right now. Also, I did make friends here. Avery (who is interesting + nice, even though she's afraid of a lot of things) + a bunch of other kids. Some of the girls in Peace Lily Pod started to cry when they found out I had to leave + this guy named Simon gave me his hoodie.

I'm not going to say good-bye to my pigs, Minnie +

Wilbur. I just can't do it. We had something really special. I can hear them squealing for me right now.

From: Daniel Birnbaum
To: Sam Bloom, Marlow Devlin
Subject: Exercising Universally Accepted Best s

Dear Mr. Bloom and Mr. Devlin,

I'm writing to you jointly as this involves both of your daughters. I made attempts to contact each of you by phone, and have left messages. I have yet to hear back from either of you.

As of the writing of this letter, Avery Bloom is off camp property and with her biological mother, Ms. Kristina Allenberry, who was not listed on the emergency form but who is clearly in the first circle of relation.

Bett Devlin is off premises, too, and is now with Betty Devlin, her grandmother (and listed emergency contact).

A full report detailing the violations of our code of conduct will be sent to both of you.

Should you have any questions do not hesitate to contact me.

Sincerely,
Daniel Birnbaum
Camp Director, CIGI

Author of *The Gifted Camper: New Approaches for the Next Generation*, published by Birnbaum House and available exclusively online

From: Avery Bloom
To: Sam Bloom
Subject: Here's what happened

Papa,

I think by now you heard about the camp problem. And probably you're really mad. But what you should be is happy, because *I'm* really, really happy.

At first I was so angry with Bett for breaking the cone of privacy. But then I saw that what makes her great is that she doesn't look at the world the way most people do. Instead, she figures things out in her own way. Sometimes that's a problem (zip line), but sometimes it's life changing, like today, which is why I'm with Kristina at the Seelocken Institute right now.

Papa, you know how you said you and Sam were having a once-in-a-lifetime experience in China? Well, that's what I'm having now.

So here's the only thing I'm asking (begging?): Could you please try to talk Bett's dad into letting Bett come here so she can be part of this once-in-a-lifetime experience, too?

Kristina says it's totally fine with her; there's plenty of room in the yurt.

Thanks, Papa. I love you so much,
Avery

From: Betty Devlin
To: Marlow Devlin
Subject: What's going on

Doug (I know you go by Marlow, but that ship has sailed for me.):

Son, your mobile phone doesn't work. I guess you know that.

So Lil' Bett got kicked out of Camp CIGI & Big Betty came to the rescue. Avery Bloom got the boot, too. It really wasn't the girls' fault, considering they were with Kristina Allenberry and she's Avery's mama. But rules are rules – this isn't Texas.

Once I got the call I jumped on the first plane, and my personal travel ban got lifted. I didn't have time to be afraid to fly, or worry that I'd get locked out of my rental car. But it cost me a bundle. We can talk about that when you're back.

I was going to drive to the camp and then back to the Detroit airport all in the same day, but Lil' Bett had another notion. She wanted to go to this place called Seelocken, which is where Avery went with her mom. Bett can be so bossy, and I was pooped from all the flying (it dries you out like a prune), so I just gave in.

Well, I'm glad I did!

You remember that I was in the Galveston Community Players all those years ago, and I did star in three of the productions? So here's what happened: Kristina Allenberry is workshopping her new play, *HOLDING UP HALF THE SKY*. That means trying it out – like cooking something new for yourself but not serving it to guests.

There was a real dust-up right when we got here because the actress Ruth Hudnutter (who plays a character named Sandra Mason) came down with an awful case of shingles & had to drop out. Kristina needed someone so they could keep blocking (that means tell you where to stand) & she asked me if I'd just be onstage and read the lines. I did that, but I took a few chances and started working the words to make them my own.

Well, when we got to the end, everyone started clapping like maniacs. Then Kristina said she'd cancel getting a replacement for Ruth Hudnutter if I'd do the part for real!

I just wish your daddy could see me. The play's having sixteen performances, so we'll be here for three weeks. But don't worry. The girls are fine. More than fine. It turns out we took lemons and we're all making lemonade!

With love from Sandra Mason
(I'm trying to stay in character)

From: Sam Bloom
To: Kristina Allenberry
Subject: Our agreement

Kristina,

What's going on? I've opened my email to an explosion of insanity. I don't hear from you for *years,* and when I do it's to say you have Avery?

Our agreement is a legally binding document. On the CIGI forms I listed Melissa Barnes, my office manager, as Avery's emergency contact. You ignored that, which is inexcusable, especially considering that Avery (AND Bett Devlin) would still be at camp IF IT WEREN'T FOR YOU.

A lot of money was spent on both girls being immersed in the arts, as well as science, technology, engineering, and maths (STEM).

Marlow and I are going to arrange to fly home as soon as we can, ending our trip early.

So I hope you're happy, Kristina. Now you've completely ruined this summer for a lot of people.

Sam

From: Bett Devlin
To: Marlow Devlin
Subject: THIS IS THE BEST SUMMER EVER

Dad,

Seelocken is the MOST AWESOME place in the world. I am not exaggerating!

Gaga said she emailed to explain everything, but just so you know, this is the opposite of CIGI, which was about finding ways to show off + impress people. Some of the classes were pretty good + I really loved Minnie + Wilbur + the horses (especially Big Mike) + the raft in the lake was fun to swim out to. Plus of course the zip line, only they closed that down.

But really, Daddy, being so smart all the time is not very relaxing.

So thank you for FORCING ME + Avery to get to KNOW each other, because as Gaga says, "We're now on a wild ride!" And you + Sam are too, only you're on motorcycles!

Love,
Betts

From: Avery Bloom
To: Sam Bloom
Subject: Seelocken

Dear Papa,

So sorry I missed your call. I had the ringer off because I don't want to wake anyone in the yurt. They stay up so late practicing their lines, or sometimes doing improv. Once they go to bed they really need their sleep.

But I did listen to your message. No, you do *not* need to be rushing home from China. *Please* don't do that. We are all doing really great here. More than really great.

So do not come home early. Stay and enjoy your romantic trip with Marlow.

Also, the secret is out: We know you two are engaged! Gaga told us that Marlow was going to pop the question, and we figure it already happened. Did it? Maybe it took place on the Great Wall. Did he get down on bended knee? I hope you both weren't near the edge of the Wall, because people can suddenly lose their balance, and a moment that's supposed to end in a wedding can end in a funeral. That's a really bad thought, but I'm not having as many of those as I used to.

We are really happy for you and also really happy for us, now that Bett and I have become close. A wedding is in our future! I've already downloaded a wedding app, which gives you checklists and timetables, with "a step-by-step, easy-to-manage alert system".

Just so you know, it says to start with the date and then work backwards. Do you have a date yet? It would help if you could get it to us ASAP.

Obviously Bett and I know we're part of the wedding party. Does that mean we'll get to be flower girls? We might be sort of old for that. Gaga (Bett's grandma) says you're never too old to get a special moment going down the aisle. I think she wants to be a flower girl, too, which is sort of crazy, but maybe she could be a Flower Older Woman, and then Bett and I could be the ones to give you guys away?

I'm just throwing out ideas here.

xo
Avery

P.S. I repeat: Do not come home from China early.

From: Sam Bloom
To: Avery Bloom
Subject: WE ARE COMING BACK EARLY

Avery,

It was very wrong of Marlow's mother "Gaga" to discuss anything with you and Bett about an engagement.

Marlow and I did exchange friendship rings when we first landed, but that was only hours after we arrived, and we were in a very emotional place, partly from the flying and the time change. We will discuss all of this when we're back.

We're now trying to get new passports (since ours were stolen) so that we can be allowed to fly home. It's not as easy as they told us. We keep waiting in very long lines for hours and hours, and then they send us to *another* office where we wait in *another* line. It's extremely frustrating.

Please turn on your phone at night in the yurt (I can't believe I just wrote that sentence) and tell Kristina to turn on her phone, too. I really have to be able to reach you when we finalize our travel plans.

Can't wait to hear your voice, babe.

Love,
Papa

From: Info@USEmbassy.China.org
To: Sam Bloom
Subject: Lost passport Case file: 198230498-B-1928473

We are processing your application. Your replacement passport may then take ten working days.

You are wearing eyeglasses in the photo you submitted. Please return to the office and submit again. Eyeglasses are not allowed.

From: Benita Ocampo
To: Bett Devlin, Avery Bloom
Subject: Hello from your friends at CIGI!

Bett & Avery –

Today, Camp Director Daniel's word of the day at morning circle was COMMUNICATION. So Petunia Pod and Peace Lily Pod decided that together we would send you guys an email, and that would be communicating in a creative way. But we aren't going to tell Camp Director Daniel, since he's been in a bad mood lately.

Here is what we want to say:

We wish you were still here.

You were fun.

We don't think it's fair that you were kicked out!

Also, Bett left a pair of red flip-flops, a tube of Kiwi Pucker-Up lip gloss, two hair clips, a sketch pad with animal drawings (really good ones, mostly pigs but some sharks and owls), and a rocket journal (apogee/altitude notes).

Avery left a pile of books with bookmarks in them. One is *Uncle Tungsten*, and one is *A Short History of Nearly Everything*, and one is *Harry Potter and the Goblet of Fire*, and the last one is *Pride and Prejudice*. She also left a tube of prescription skin cream (hydrocortisone 0.5%), nasal spray, and about a thousand Band-Aids.

Write back and tell us where Benita should send the stuff, and what you're both doing. Bett, are you in Texas? Avery, did you get to stay with your mom?

Love from Stella, Lauri, Dyllan, Charlotte R., Charlotte M., Charlotte P., Emma, Hannah, Sibi, Ava, Solana, Annie, Zoe, LeeLing, Pari, and Dilshad.

P.S. This is Benita's personal email. She can be trusted.

From: Bett Devlin
To: Benita Ocampo
Subject: Re: CIGI podmates

Hi, Stella, Lauri, Dyllan, Charlotte R., Charlotte M., Charlotte P., Emma, Hannah, Sibi, Ava, Solana, Annie, Zoe, LeeLing, Pari + Dilshad –

It's Bett + Avery writing from Bett's email.

Guess what? We're TOGETHER at Seelocken. It's eighty-five miles from CIGI but it feels like we're on another PLANET!

We miss you guys but we're super happy we got kicked out because this place is an INSTITUTE, which turns out to be the ADULT word for CAMP.

They only have ONE activity, which is putting on a play + it takes up everyone's time. But we're NOT in the play + we aren't making costumes or designing scenery so we get to do whatever we want + that means DRIVE!

Yes, drive.

We have OUR OWN GOLF CART! You read that right!

Here at the Institute we eat whenever we want + we don't have any lights-out time or wake-up time. We sleep in a big yurt. They have 6 of them. The adults sleep LATE, which is totally cool.

Here are the things that have happened to us in the last week:

1. Everyone went swimming at 2:00 a.m. Avery only went in up to her waist + didn't swim, but she still had the experience + she can't believe she was in a lake at NIGHT, which is probably the scariest thing she's ever done in her life + why she was screaming the whole time.

2. We picked wild blueberries. The first 7 minutes were fun. The second 7 minutes were sort of boring. The next 2 minutes were just work + then we quit. So if someone asks you to go find wild blueberries, remember this time breakdown.

3. We cooked DINNER for the whole camp. It was our idea. They gave us money + we took the golf cart to buy food at the store in the town that's close by. We wore bike helmets + drove in the grass next to the breakdown lane of the big highway! BUT IT WAS ONLY FOR 1 EXIT + VERY VERY SAFE. Cars honked + people waved at us!

It's a lot harder to make dinner for 65 people than you'd think. We didn't have enough food, but people were okay about it (it's not easy to figure out portions for large groups). We served salad, bread, and spaghetti with lemon cream sauce since we didn't want to have a meat dish plus a vegetarian option because that would be cooking 2 dinners.

We use nicknames here a lot. Avery is Night Owl + Bett is Dogfish. We call ourselves those nicknames because the actors all use their character names. Well, when the meal we cooked was over, everyone stood + clapped and SOME people even shouted "Yay, Night Owl! Yay, Dogfish!" It was awesome. We came out of the kitchen + took a bow.

But we're NOT going to cook a big meal like this again. Zesting so many lemons hurts your arm. Also we ran out of spaghetti in the middle so we had to hand out egg salad sandwiches with dessert + the next day no one could have omelets at breakfast.

Here's more stuff that's been GREAT: No one asks us if we are wearing sunscreen or bug spray. Or if we brushed our teeth or flossed. (Just so you know, WE DO wear sunscreen + sometimes bug spray + we mostly brush our teeth. We never floss.) Also, Bett eats pepperoni pizza EVERY single day for lunch and dinner + doesn't get lectured about eating all the food groups in the pyramid.

Another thing that's happening: Our dads are GETTING MARRIED – but that's still a secret. This means we will be sisters! And at the wedding we might be flower girls. But we could also each be the best man, which would be renamed the best woman. All of this is still to be figured out. But we're very, very excited about it, which is a big change from how we felt in the beginning, when we were upset after our dads started going out.

Okay, thanks for writing, CIGIES! If this place had a slogan it would be: CAMP WITHOUT RULES IS THE BEST CAMP OF ALL.

Cheers! (That's what the actress here from London says about 20 times a day.)

Bett + Avery

P.S. Hi, Counsellor Benita + Counsellor Rachel. Thanks for reading this out loud to all our friends. Press DELETE when you are done. Camp Director Daniel might have spyware.

Also, can you send the stuff we left in the pods (lip gloss, etc.) to the main office at Seelocken? We go in there about 10 times a day to get money for the candy machine + also for ice. The address is online.

From: Avery Bloom
To: Sam Bloom
Subject: Take your time

Papa –

Everyone has to have phones off in the theatre, so that's why I missed your call again. But I got your voicemail message saying you're having trouble getting new passports. I really wish we could help you guys! Kristina says that you both should take this time to do more travelling in China while you're waiting for the new passports to come through.

If you leave another message on my phone, could you give us an idea of the wedding date?

Love you,
Avery

From: Bett Devlin
To: Marlow Devlin
Subject: Learning lots every day!

Dad,

I feel like I'm LEARNING a lot here. So even though I'm not at CIGI that money wasn't all wasted.

Also, Gaga's NOT the star of the play, but she IS the star of this whole place! They call her Lady Gaga. She LOVES it. Kristina keeps making Gaga's part BIGGER + BIGGER by writing more lines (some of them come right from Gaga but she's not going to take any credit for that).

I didn't know until now that she was even an actress!

Me + Avery watch rehearsals but Kristina gave us her golf cart (since her driver, Ben, went back to Ohio for good). We just need to pick up Kristina when she wants to go places + mostly she's in the theatre.

Avery's driven a few times, only she's really afraid of crashing + killing us. She went off the path once because she saw a very cute bunny + the cart ran over a sprinkler, which broke + sent water everywhere.

But they have a plumbing guy here so it got fixed right away. Also, they aren't so worried about water like in California, which made it not as much of a problem.

I want you to know we DO NOT take the cart on the big road. We drive ONLY on the trails + also we use the cart to cut across the field to get to the lake.

I wish we lived here, Daddy. Especially if we had a golf cart, + we could just sign for food whenever we wanted, which is what we do at the snack bar.

Avery eats very healthy but I'm not going to lie because I do get pepperoni pizza every now + then. You would, too, if you were here. The cheese is from Wisconsin + they know what they're doing there.

Gaga says this is our time to be FREE + it's also her time to be FREE. Please be FREE in China with Sam.

So don't rush back. Seriously, take your time + go see fun stuff + sleep in late + go bowling if they have that there. There should be no hurrying when it comes to love.

So that's it. Miss you. As in forever. (That's what me + Avery say to each other as our code for just about everything.)

Love you, Daddy.
Betty Jr.

From: Betty Devlin
To: Diamond Johnson
Subject: Thanks for taking care of stuff for me

Diamond –

I know it can't be any fun watering my yard. Or getting my mail. But I bet Cinnamon doesn't miss me a bit. They say that cats like you when you're there, but then don't care if you move to another time zone as long as someone's putting Meow Mix in the bowl. You're a saint for taking her to your place. Whisper in her little ear that her mama's missing her.

I've been away from home now for two whole weeks, but it feels like two months. Only in a good way. The longest days but the shortest weeks, if you know what I mean. I'm on my feet for hours onstage working on this play. I'm not going to pretend it's a job because it's nothing like that. It's just plain fun.

Bett is growing up so fast. And Avery (looks like she'll be my new grandchild!) has warmed up to me in a big way. She's a good influence on Bett, who can be a wild and difficult child. Avery tries to put the brakes on at all times. She's got plenty of fears and she's a first-class worrier like an old lady, but she's smart and makes me laugh. Even though she's from a big city, she's not too full of herself. They make a great team.

At first I was worried that Dougie would show up with his fiancé, Sam, and take the girls away (I'd already decided I was staying here even if that happened – I'm in a play and they need me), but the men lost their passports and they have to get new ones. Every day they make a bigger mess of things for themselves. It doesn't sound like much fun to me, but then again flying halfway around the world seemed nuts, especially because they hadn't been a couple for very long. They could have gone on a fishing trip up the Delta and had an easier time of it.

Of course if they'd done that, I wouldn't be sleeping with my grandbabies by a blue-green lake in Michigan! I wouldn't be learning how to do vocal exercises and eating tofu scramble. (I can hear you laughing, but it doesn't taste half bad, Diamond, just so you know.) I wouldn't be able to sing all the words to the play *Hamilton* or be turning into a board game geek! You've got to try Forbidden Island.

Everyone wants to be a big shot nowadays and have pictures of themselves to put up on the Internet. I always thought it was just a lot of showing off. But now I'm getting ready to update my Facebook page for the first time in years. I'm in a play, and people should know about it.

Shine on!

Betty (known here only as Gaga)

P.S. It's such a gift to have this much alone time with Lil' Bett. I've been filling her in on family stuff and such. She's a sponge for it all.

From: Bett Devlin
To: Avery Bloom
Subject: Stuff Gaga told ME that Kristina told HER

Hey, Night Owl –

I'm with Gaga right now in town + she's getting her feet checked by a doctor because of bunions, which is the most boring thing I've ever written to someone. Or ANYONE has ever written to someone. I'll be back in an hour. Don't get ice cream without me.

While I've been stuck here, Gaga told me some fun stories about my dad when he was a kid. And she also told me some of YOUR ORIGIN STORY, which I'm sure you know, but I might have some new facts that you haven't heard before. Kristina tells Gaga everything personal.

Anyway, Gaga said that Kristina + your dad were BEST FRIENDS all through college + your dad was discovering he was gay. But they had one crazy night + Kristina GOT PREGNANT.

Kristina decided to keep the baby (YOU) + then her mom (your grandma SUSAN) told Kristina that she'd help raise you in the early years, so that Kristina could go to London where she had won a place in some big-deal theatre company.

Your dad was freaked out by everything + went to start architect school in New York.

But then at the end of your second year of life, your grandma Susan DIED of a stroke (which came out of nowhere! She got a big headache one day. But you should NOT worry about that happening to you. Most headaches are nothing!). Kristina flew to Ohio + they had a funeral + your dad came + Kristina fell apart.

So your dad decided to finally take being a parent seriously + he packed up all kinds of baby stuff + drove you + Kristina BOTH to New York. They didn't have any kind of plan.

Only Kristina had to get back to London soon + you got an ear infection + the doctor said you SHOULDN'T FLY.

So Kristina went to London alone, thinking she'd be back in 3 weeks, but she slipped on the icy sidewalk in front of the theatre + broke her ankle + she had to have surgery + she couldn't travel for 4 MORE months.

You were with your dad that whole time + when Kristina finally got to you in New York you hadn't seen her in half a year + you didn't even know who she was! She took you to a park + a dog knocked you over + bit you on the lip. You had to have stitches! Kristina thought it all meant that she was a horrible mom.

So she + your dad went to a therapist who said maybe your dad should have sole (or soul?) custody because it would be less confusing for you than going back + forth all the time to London.

Kristina said okay. But she now knows that the moment she said "Okay" she had made the biggest mistake of her life. If she could turn back the hands of time + change anything, that would be the ONE thing she would do. She said that signing over custody of you broke her heart.

So whenever you see someone standing on a bridge in one of her plays crying, like in *TELL ME WHEN JIMMY COMES HOME*, or on a roof crying, or anywhere else, they are really crying about YOU. They are crying because they lost the most valuable thing they ever had. Not that you are a "thing". But you know what she means.

Anyway, Gaga said NOT TO TELL YOU THIS. But I decided to go in a different direction.

Love,
Dogfish

From: Avery Bloom
To: Bett Devlin
Subject: Re: Stuff Gaga told ME that Kristina told HER

This is super upsetting and I feel like I've been looking through the keyhole of a door into a room that is my own life, and before now I could only see some of it. Now the door is open at least a crack. There are two major things that I hadn't known before.

1) No one ever told me that Kristina was heartbroken. I've just thought of her as a busy playwright who had her own life in England. I feel like she could have found a way

to be in touch with me. Did my papa stop her from doing that? Or is she now rewriting the past? (She *is* a writer.)

2) Also, I never knew that Kristina was in the park with me when the big dog knocked me down and bit me. That story's just been about me and a bad dog experience. I always assumed my dad was with me. And the funny thing is that it's so far in the past, it's faded away into an explanation about why I have that little scar on my lip. I'm afraid of deep water a lot more than dogs.

I'm thinking now that maybe all stories are there to explain something.

I really like reading stories with an unreliable narrator, because the person telling you what happened can't be trusted with the facts and you have to figure it out.

Maybe when it's your own story, you're always going to be an unreliable narrator.

SENT as TEXT MESSAGE

Girls—You're not going to believe what's happening! It's about to be announced online. You must be some-where in the golf cart—oh wait, I can see you over the hill—

PLAYBILL.COM LEAD STORY

The latest announcement out of Seelocken, Michigan, is that the summer production of Tony-nominated and Drama Desk Award-winning playwright Kristina Allenberry's newest work, *HOLDING UP HALF THE SKY*, is headed for an off-Broadway run in the spring.

Planned for a February preview with a March start at New World Stages, #4, the production will feature cast member (and newcomer) Betty Hawkins Devlin in the role of Sandra Mason.

Other parts will be recast, with rumours swirling that Auli'i Cravalho is in talks to play the lead, Sister Elaine. Reps confirmed Nia Long is in early negotiations for the part of Ruthie Hocks.

Valeria Garcia directs the twelve-actor piece, which explores time and identity. Martina DeSouza will provide sound design. Dilly Clark is in charge of moving light programming.

From: Avery Bloom
To: The Hon. Evan Balakian
Subject: Booking a date for a wedding

Dear Judge Balakian,

I asked Ariel for your email address. She wrote back one word: "Why?" I told her the answer, and now I'll tell you (but maybe don't share it because it's not yet on Instagram or any social media, and a lot of people make announcements now with engagement photos).

My papa's getting married! For a while I was the only kid in our class with a gay parent, though it's great that it's not that way anymore since Maddy Burkett showed up with her two moms (and all those cats), and then Will Garrd's dad left his mom for Will's science tutor.

Anyway, Ariel said you sometimes marry people. So I'm writing to ask if you'd marry my papa and his new partner, D. Marlow Devlin. He and my papa are in China right now, exploring the open road (on motorcycles, which is very dangerous, but very exciting for them).

Marlow's daughter, Bett, has been with me at camp in Michigan (and now at a theatre programme at the Seelocken Institute) and is my new best friend. Please tell Ariel she will always be my *oldest* best friend, as well as my *school* best friend. Bett and I can't wait to be sisters. (Legally, stepsisters.)

I know how busy my papa is (I have his Google calendar for the fall synced with my phone), so I thought I would take care of this while he's away and surprise him and Marlow when they get back.

Would you consider officiating at their wedding, now that the Supreme Court's decision on gay marriage has made the world more fair?

Some possible dates that could work are: 7/9, 12/10, 13/10, 19/10, 20/10.

Probably it would be an afternoon wedding followed

by a dinner with long table seating and a possible "small animals of the world" theme. (Bett's idea.)

If you could commit to this, it would be a big thing to check off the list. If you can't do it, I totally understand. Ariel said you like to golf on weekends.

Please say hello to Ariel's mom for me and tell her I can't wait to eat her flax pancakes this fall on a sleepover. My about-to-be new sister, Bett, is a big pancake person, and says she really wants to meet Ariel, especially when she found out you guys have a schnoodle. Bett loves dogs and says she's never spent any time with a schnauzer-poodle mix.

I hope you and your family are having an amazing summer.

Sincerely,
Avery Bloom

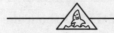

From: Bett Devlin
To: Marlow Devlin
Subject: Explaining about the tractor

Dad – I want to explain that if you see a picture of me online DRIVING A TRACTOR (with Avery squeezed next to me in the seat) it's not REALLY real.

I mean, it's not photoshopped or anything + yes, I'm driving, but the tractor is moving VERY SLOWLY + we are in the field at Seelocken just doing that FOR A PICTURE on our last day here because the tractor is so big + the whole thing looks funny. It was VERY windy, so that's why my hair is blowing back like that.

I realized when Rena (who does publicity for the plays) said she was putting the picture on the theatre website, you might see us. But probably not. Gaga is here + of course she knows all about heavy farm equipment + it was very very SAFE. That's why we have on those hard hats.

Also, Avery is screaming in the photo the way you scream on a roller coaster. (She has actually never been on one, but if she had, she would have screamed like that.) Her expression is from GOOD SCREAMING. You can ask her. Or have her dad ask her. But if he hasn't seen the picture – why bother?

Okay, that's me checking in. Also, did you know that most tractors have 4 forward speeds with a high + low range? You start with the P.T.O. + that means Power Take Off.

At CIGI they just TALKED about mechanical stuff, but at drama camp it's REAL.

We all leave for New York tomorrow. Empty your voicemail. It's full + that's freaking out Gaga. She's got LOTS OF NEWS.

We're glad you stayed + didn't come racing back home even if you were TRYING to come racing back home but failed because of not having passports.

Love you,
Bett

From: Betty Devlin
To: Marlow Devlin
Subject: Seelocken

Doug –

We keep missing your calls. But the ten-hour time change isn't helping, and also the Institute is in the woods and phone signal isn't what it should be, so our phones don't ring half the time. We just see the messages afterwards. Sorry, son.

Here at Seelocken we're almost done with the play (fastest three weeks of my life) & now we're all going to go together to New York City.

I'm guessing you just spit out your coffee – or probably your tea. You know I don't travel & I've only been to New York once & that was during the Jimmy Carter administration, but this is a business trip for me. You read that right: a business trip.

I was hoping to tell you the news in person, but we are taking the play *HOLDING UP HALF THE SKY* to off-Broadway. By "we" I mean I'm part of it!

It's not happening till the spring, but I need to find somewhere to stay in New York City (even though Avery keeps saying we're a family now & there's room for us in the Bloom apartment). Kristina lives in London, but she's going to get a little New York spot now, too.

Another reason I'm flying east is because I'm meeting

with an agent. He saw the play & he wants to "represent" me. First I thought that was fishy, but Kristina says that this man, Emerson Morgan, is for real and I will need him to negotiate my contract.

Mercy me, everything's spinning in new directions. Okay, honey – we'll try your mobile when we're at the airport in Detroit. They must get better reception there.

Love you to death –

Your mama (or Sandra Mason. She's kind of unpredictable but has guts.)

From: Sam Bloom
To: Avery Bloom
Subject: Finally got a flight

Okay, we got temporary passports and I'm finally on a plane to NYC. We board in thirty minutes. The flight takes twenty-five hours, stopping in Dallas. I still can't believe it took this long to get out of here.

I can't wait to see you, Ave. We have so much catching up to do. So much has happened to each of us.

One day in the far-off future I'm hoping that I have a sense of humour about it all.

Love from,
Your Papa

P.S. I'm sending the flight details to my office. I'll text you when I land. Let Kristina know that I expect to find you waiting for me at home. She didn't return my last two emails. It's best if you get Dee to watch you. I don't think I'll be in any mood to see Kristina.

From: Marlow Devlin
To: Betty Devlin
Subject: Flying back home

Mom –

I'll be back in LA tomorrow. I know you said you were in New York, but I need you to get on a flight with Bett and be in LA when I arrive.

I have a lot to tell you, but I don't want to put some of it in writing. Especially because Bett gets into my email.

See you soon.
Marlow

From: Betty Devlin
To: Marlow Devlin
Subject: Seelocken

We've got a flight to LA, and we'll be there to meet you when you arrive. Don't worry about paying for the flights, because I got a cross-country trip in my play contract and it includes what they call a "plus one." (Bett.)

We're packing up now. And you probably know this, but the Blooms' NY apartment is as fancy as I've seen. Bett took a lot of pictures.

See you soon, sugar.

From: Bett Devlin
To: Avery Bloom
Subject: FIRST CLASS FLYING

I'm on the plane. In FIRST CLASS, which is like you said "AWESOME" but probably really bad for a person because who wants to fly the old, cramped, uncomfortable way once you've done this?

It's another thing that shows how people live in the same world only a different one, but at the same time. Up front there was champagne (I got orange juice) as soon as we walked on. They hung up our coats + couldn't stop smiling, while behind us most of the other people had to squeeze down the aisle while getting yelled at to take their seats as quickly as possible.

Gaga said they looked afraid that they were going to be kicked off the plane because of overbooking. They can see our bathroom but were told not to use it, which makes me feel bad. But the flight attendant closed our little curtain so they can't see in.

Right now they're baking us fresh chocolate chip cookies. Behind the curtain a baby is crying. At least I hope it's a baby.

Gaga keeps saying she doesn't know the first thing about being an actress + she didn't even understand half of Kristina's play. I told her we never stayed for the whole thing because it wasn't meant for kids + also it was more fun to be out running around on our own.

Remember the owls? (Of course you do, Night Owl.) I loved them so much. I wish we could have trained the ones in the trees to fly down + land on our shoulders. (We could have even had one in the wedding ceremony, maybe swooping down with the rings tied with ribbons to its claws!)

Gaga says that too much travelling can make a person crazy. I don't know if she's talking about my dad or herself because she just emptied a dish of warm nuts into her coin purse.

This trip to China was hard on the dads, but they will be SO happy when they hear that we got along great + that we're fine with them getting married. We were such pains about it in the beginning.

I really really can't wait to start my own dog-walking business if we move to New York. I bet I'll make a fortune. But maybe they'll decide that it's not fair to pick one of the cities over the other + that means living halfway instead, so we'll be 1 big family somewhere in Oklahoma. They have a good basketball team there.

I'll report back once we've landed + we get Junie + Raisin home from the kennel in Topanga.

More soon!
xo
Dogfish Devlin-Bloom

From: Avery Bloom
To: Bett Devlin
Subject: Disaster

I tried to call! You didn't answer! Where are you? Something bad happened. Something really, really horrible.

Papa gets back from China, and right away things are weird. At first we just sit in the kitchen and talk about nothing. I know he's mad about me going with Kristina to Seelocken, but he isn't even bringing that up. He has other things on his mind. So finally he says, "I need to tell you something important."

But then he can't look at me.

He turns away and I see his left leg jiggling, which is a nervous thing he does. From the look on his face I know this is something really, truly terrible. So I start to cry. He hasn't even said a word yet, and I'm already sobbing. Finally he says to me:

"Marlow and I have decided to give things a rest."

I don't get it at first. I say, "You mean you're so tired from the jet lag and everything, that you both need to nap?"

So then he says no, that's not what he means. He says the trip was very stressful, and he and your dad are very different, and they didn't get along at all. Everything turned into an argument. He says they couldn't stop fighting. They need for this relationship to be over. And he paces around the kitchen, and he even picks up a wooden spoon and starts waving it in the air.

I finally say, "What are you talking about? What are you telling me?"

He says, "We broke up. It's over. Done."

And then he leaves the room.

Now I can't stop crying. I didn't know I had so many tears inside me. I guess the body makes tears on an as-needed basis. I lay down on Marshmallow Fluff and pushed my face into the leather (which is bad because it's not supposed to get wet, and also it's hard to breathe), and I used up a whole travel pack of Kleenex with aloe.

Papa said your dad was giving you the bad news at the same time. I mean three hours earlier, where you are. Eastern Time and then Pacific Time. Just like when they both were going to give us the CIGI T-shirts, except of course this is a lot worse.

Did you get the same speech? Dad says he thought I'd be fine with the breakup. He thought I didn't want our family to change. He doesn't understand about you and me. That makes it even worse.

He's in his room, so I called Kristina, who says I need to understand that he's in pain right now and not thinking clearly. I don't want to be a big narcissist, but *I'm* in *horrible pain* right now, too (but thinking clearly).

Does this mean our dads won't ever be husbands? They won't get married? There won't be a wedding? Is it really possible we'll never know what our lives would've been like all together as a family?

Tonight I'm going to have full-blown insomnia – not just my usual night owl thing – which can become a chronic condition if not properly treated.

Nothing was missing before in my life, but now it will be. You will be.

Night Owl and Dogfish won't ever be together. That just can't be true.

From: Bett Devlin
To: Avery Bloom
Subject: Re: Disaster

What??? NO!!! We're just getting started. Aren't they ENGAGED + aren't we PLANNING A WEDDING? Don't you have that special wedding planner app? Didn't he have a ring on his finger? Didn't you order 3 different wedding books for research + put your friend's judge dad on hold?

I need to hear what my dad says.

We're going to the airport to get him in 4 hours. His

flight was delayed so the "telling us both at the same time" thing didn't work, if that was really their plan.

I'm not going to tell Gaga anything + I'm not going to cry, either, because right now we only have 1 side to this story.

I would Skype with you, but Gaga would hear + she's already acting completely nuts realizing she's actually going to be in a play in New York in the spring. She's in the living room right now doing her new vocal exercises (it's a lot of vowel sounds soft then loud over and over and over again). It's making the dogs howl.

From: Evan Balakian
To: Avery Bloom
Re: Save the date request

Avery,

I was very touched to get your email last week, and I would be honored to marry your father and his new life partner. A formal (and legal) union of two people in a personal relationship is cause for great celebration. Congratulations!

I'm holding the first two weekends in October open for your family. Let me know as soon as you can which date is best and we will make it a firm booking.

All best to this new adventure!
Judge Evan

P.S. I'll of course waive my standard fee for you guys! (Wondering, though, if your dad would have a brief look at some blueprints for our weekend house in Bedford. We are using an architect from McClain, Strothers, but he's young and not that experienced. Maybe your dad could weigh in?)

From: Bett Devlin
To: Avery Bloom
Subject: THEY ARE BIG IDIOTS

Night Owl –

Dad is home.
It's true. THEY BROKE UP.
Dad said that he + your dad LOVED each other, but travelling together made them not LIKE each other. They're too different, he said.
Then he cried. He got in the front seat of his pickup truck in the parking lot at the airport + then he let Gaga drive + he cried. He NEVER LETS GAGA DRIVE + I've only seen him cry at movies + sad TV + when the Supreme Court ruled that same-sex couples had a right to be married – but that last one was HAPPY CRYING.
That's not how he cried today. And once he started

crying Gaga lost it, too. She sucked her whole bottom lip into her mouth + she was swearing at the same time she was sobbing. I put my hands over my face so that I couldn't see them + then out of nowhere, RAISIN BIT JUNIE.

This has NEVER happened before. Raisin LOVES Junie. I think all of us crying in a small place (Dad's pickup truck) was a TRIGGER. We know she came from a negative environment.

Raisin had Junie's only good ear + Dad had to dive into the back + try to pull them apart. I grabbed the truck door handle and opened it (which I shouldn't have done because we were moving).

Gaga SCREAMED. But we didn't crash. We hit the kerb + an airport policewoman was there + she ordered Gaga out of the truck. We pulled Raisin + Junie apart + got them on the SIDEWALK where it was like nothing had happened except a whole chunk of dog ear was now missing. Maybe Raisin swallowed it. We don't know.

Then, while we untangled the leads, Raisin tried to lick Junie's face.

I think it's an OMEN. It means that your dad + my dad got into some kind of fight, but after they're away from each other they'll want to be together again.

We didn't take Junie to the vet because the ear stopped bleeding with pressure (my sock, Dad's fingers) + she doesn't have much of a flap on the other side, so it almost looks like more of a match now.

I don't get it: Why can't the dads be different but also be together? Look at you + me. We're really different but we get along great most of the time.

I feel very very very SAD. We're all going to bed + Gaga said that the sun will come out tomorrow. But my dad's eyes are heartbroken.

So are mine.

I never even met Sam Bloom.

I never even got to MEET YOUR PAPA.

xo
LOVE, Dogfish

From: Avery Bloom
To: Bett Devlin
Subject: Re: THEY ARE BIG IDIOTS

I'm not supposed to check my phone or read email when I'm trying to sleep, because as I've told you it's really bad sleep hygiene, and I have trouble falling asleep, and also falling back to sleep if I wake up in the night, which is something I do way more than is good for me. But all the rules are now broken. Even the one about run-on sentences.

Call me tomorrow the minute you wake up.

From: Bett Devlin
To: Kristina Allenberry
Subject: We are NOT going to be a FAMILY

Kristina –

Did you hear the news that we aren't going to be a family? My dad + Avery's dad broke up in China. They couldn't get along.

We can't blame the lost passports, or the broken-down motorcycle (even though none of that helped).

We can't blame our dads, because we love them.

Also, they feel as bad as we do.

Maybe they feel worse.

But I feel pretty awful.

Only it's not a contest to see who's feeling it most.

Gaga says that our lives got bigger because of their love. It's true. I went to CIGI + then to Seelocken + I drove a golf cart + a tractor on all 4 speeds. Avery + I swam in the lake (well, I swam + she got in the water, which is a big deal for her). We made not enough lemon spaghetti for everyone + slept in a yurt + tried to train owls using salami + it worked a little bit. Avery gave me a book + I read half of it.

Me + Gaga got to be together this summer + fly in seats 2A + 2B across the country, which means first class, with tickets paid for by the theatre company.

We looked for shooting stars every night + sometimes we saw them.

No one can take that away because it HAPPENED.

It isn't a contest to see who feels the worst.

There are no winners in that game.

I hope we can stay friends, even if we aren't going to be family.

Love,
Bett Devlin, also known as Dogfish

From: Kristina Allenberry
To: Bett Devlin
Subject: Re: We are NOT going to be a FAMILY

Bett –

I still want you in my family no matter what happens with your dad and Sam. This summer gave me back my daughter, Avery. You set that in motion. And an object in motion is hard to stop, because it picks up speed as it goes along. Sweet Bett, all families have broken parts, so that makes us like everyone else, special in our own messy way.

Love from the mother of your chosen sister, which makes you another daughter of mine.

Your Kristina

From: Avery Bloom
To: Kristina Allenberry
cc: Bett Devlin
Subject: Us

Dear Kristina,

Bett forwarded me the email you sent her. I don't see how it's true that we can all be a family. My dad doesn't even want me to talk to you.

I know we had this amazing summer. But people in a family (even if they don't live together) spend time with each other. They share stuff. Up until now, you and I haven't done that.

If you want to be a parent, you have to do a lot of things that aren't as fun or interesting as what we did at Seelocken. Like you'd have to help me study my Latin and French vocabulary cards. Also, I get very worried before tests. And I need a lot of emotional support before anything with geometry.

There are other things. I do a lot of checking on the sell-by dates of foods. (Sell-by dates are very important. But they shouldn't be confused with use-by dates.) Also, I can get very worried about dying. I watch too much of the Weather Channel when there's a storm alert, even one that's not in our area. I read books when I'm supposed to be asleep. I use cotton buds every day in my ears, not just on the rim. I don't like thunder. Escalators. Rope ladders. Dented cans. Paper lampshades that are too close to the lightbulbs, which can get hot very fast. Teflon pans where the protective surface has been scratched. (It causes cancer.) And, of course, I have that fear-of-drowning problem, which means I don't like swimming pools or ponds, rivers, lakes, and oceans.

What I'm really asking is do you want to see me enough

to put up with all of that? Would you live in New York City? And if you did, would that be in a hotel or an apartment?

Would the hotel have room service?

And a clearly marked fire exit?

Could I go there after school?

I know that you're always travelling, but if you were in my life now, would there be a place for us to call home?

Love,
Avery

From: Sam Bloom
To: Marlow Devlin
Subject: Deconstruction

You and I decided it was best to not communicate, but some issues have come up. Avery has become very attached to Bett. Maybe "dependent" is a better word.

Avery also expresses a desire to see *your* mother, Betty (who she calls "Gaga").

This summer was very traumatic for Avery. And also for me. What I'm trying to say is I want to move forward in a way that eases us back into our former lives. The girls were on Skype yesterday for over an hour. Not healthy.

I need your help untangling this mess and setting boundaries for the kids.

SB

From: Marlow Devlin
To: Sam Bloom
Subject: Re: Deconstruction

Sam, we've been saying that our passports were stolen. But we both know that YOU think it happened because I wasn't paying attention and left my bag in the hotel. We both thought a trip to China would be great. But then I added in the motorcycle part because I've always wanted to travel that way. So now all our problems there were MY fault.

I make mistakes, Sam. I admit that. I guess you were one of them.

As far as our daughters are concerned, we forced them to meet. They had nothing in common except us. We told them that they were going to be sisters. Then we said they weren't. They SHOULD be confused. They SHOULD have things to talk over. I'm not getting in the middle of that.

From: Sam Bloom
To: Marlow Devlin
Subject: RE: re: Deconstruction

Avery and Bett live 3,000 miles away from each other, and they will make other friends, and you and I will meet other people, too.

That's how it works. Continuing contact isn't good – for us or for them. I'm sorry you don't get that.

To speed things up on my end, I've unfriended you on Facebook, plus I've stopped following you on Instagram, so feel free to post whatever you like. And I'll take you out of my phone contacts – so no text messaging.

My life and my family have nothing to do anymore with your life and your family. I hope I've made this all clear.

From: Marlow Devlin
To: Sam Bloom
Subject: Re: re: re: Deconstruction

VERY.

From: Betty Devlin
To: Marlow Devlin
Subject: In NYC

Doug –

I arrived back in New York safe and sound. Kristina came to the airport to meet me, which made all the difference. We're now looking for rental places near each other. We've got to be together in this city if I'm doing the play next spring, or I won't be able to handle it.

Write to me with an update when you get a chance. I've got my fingers crossed that you and Sam are finding a way to build a solid friendship!

Love and much more love,
Gaga

From: Bett Devlin
To: Betty Devlin
Subject: YOU'RE A CELEBRITY!!!!!!

Gaga –

I showed everybody at school the announcement about your PLAY in the *New York Times*. Dad says we'll frame it. I let my friends + also Mrs Kleinsasser + Mr Yip see the article + I posted it online so people will know you're my grandma. We're all really proud of you.

I want to say Dad is doing a lot better because he's trying to act like he's back to normal, but I can tell he's just pretending.

If I get up in the middle of the night to go to the bathroom he's usually on the couch. Not asleep. Just sitting looking at stuff. One time he didn't hear me come in + I saw he was staring at pictures from China on his iPad. It's mostly him and Sam standing next to their motorcycles, with fields or mountains or cities in the background. In some of them their arms are around each other.

I'm in touch with Avery every day. We send text messages or we Skype + we try to write each other a real email at least once a week.

I miss her A LOT. I didn't even know her before the summer + I didn't want her for a friend (I had enough friends + she didn't seem like friend material) + now I can't imagine not having her as part of everything.

I don't know if you heard that Kristina + Sam Bloom are fighting like wolverines (as you like to say). I tried to bring it up a few times with Dad, but he doesn't want to know. That's what he says: "I don't want to know." Then he waves his hand, like, stop talking about it right this second.

Our plan is to go to New York to see you in the play when it opens in March.

Love you, Gaga!
xo
Lil' Betty

From: Avery Bloom
To: Bett Devlin
Subject: More trouble

Dogfish –

Papa went out and left his laptop open, so I looked. I invaded his privacy. I copied this email below and sent it to myself. I'm now forwarding it to you. This is bad.

Night Owl

From: The Law Offices of King, McElroy, Watson & Peacor LLP
To: Sam Bloom
Subject: Avery Allenberry Bloom

Dear Mr Bloom,

I represent Ms Kristina Allenberry.

Ms Allenberry acknowledges that a document was signed ten years ago but she now seeks fifty per cent (50%) physical custody of her biological daughter, Avery Allenberry Bloom, currently residing with you at 2211 Broadway, New York, New York 10024.

My office will be contacting you to set up an appointment to discuss this situation.

Sincerely,
Ryan King
Partner, King, McElroy, Watson & Peacor LLP

From: Bett Devlin
To: Avery Bloom
Subject: Spying

Night Owl –

All I can say is WOW. They are going to fight over you. This is really serious. Send me every detail. I may be on the other side of the country, but I'm there for you.

Also, because of the time difference I'm up REALLY late your time. I'm basically your crisis hotline.

Dogfish

From: Avery Bloom
To: Bett Devlin
Subject: Big Trouble

Dogfish,

It's only getting worse. Papa got home and called Kristina and started shouting about custody. I had poster board left over from last year's Irish Immigration project, and in alternating purple and orange letters I wrote YOU ARE BEING MEAN TO MY BIOLOGICAL MOM!!!! I came into the room holding up my sign while loudly humming. That made him hang up.

But he didn't calm down. He turned to me and shouted, "Stop humming!" So I did. Then he took my sign right out of my hands and said, "Did Bett Devlin, of the famous zip-line incident, who got in touch with Kristina without asking anyone and has an equally reckless dad, tell you to make this ridiculous sign? Because guess what? You are not allowed to speak to Bett ever again! She's a terrible influence on you!"

I couldn't believe how mean he was being about you and your dad. But I also couldn't believe he thought I couldn't make a sign without help.

I think this was the first time I really stood up to him. There wasn't ever a reason to do it before, but now that he's acting like a different person he's making it easy.

You and I are now the Romeo and Juliet of friendship. Only we're the Juliet and Juliet.

This is very, very stressful. It's possible I can feel my cortisol levels actually rising. Unsure.

xx
Night Owl

From: Kristina Allenberry
To: Avery Bloom
Subject: Heads UP!

Avery –

I want you to know that your papa and I are doing some back and forth with legal help about your schedule. We're not fighting, even if it looks like we are. It's just the way the system works. It's designed to turn discussion into a hassle so that the people who spent three years in law school can pay off their student loans.

But there's nothing to worry about. I'll see you on Tuesday and we'll go out for dessert, and even go to the medical supply store that you like. (I agree that just looking at the equipment sounds interesting.)

Love you,
Kristina

P.S. I signed the lease for the apartment (only four blocks away from you), and Gaga got a place in the same building, on the same floor! We'll soon all be New Yorkers!

From: Bett Devlin
To: Avery Bloom
Subject: Spying Again

Night Owl –

Dad's out working, so I decided to see what he's been up to by checking his email. Here's something interesting: It turns out that Kristina has been in touch with him!

Did you give her my dad's email address? I guess it's "the enemy of my enemy is my friend".

People think that Captain Kirk said that in a Star Trek movie, which is true, but FIRST it was said by CHANAKYA, who was an Indian man in the 4th Century BC. I know because we're doing a project at school called "Give the right person the credit". A lot of women + minorities have lost out in the past.

xo
Dogfish

P.S. Pro-tip: If you want to get your dad more on your side use your inhaler a lot. He will feel sorry for you.

From: Avery Bloom
To: Bett Devlin
Subject: Re: Spying Again

I didn't know about Chanakya. And yes, Kristina wanted your dad's contact info. Of course I shared!

I think that the common enemies communicating is good. My update is that a social worker's been assigned to "evaluate my home environment" for the custody thing. Both at my *real* home with Papa, and at the apartment Kristina just rented. So things are really getting out of control.

Report back. I'm pretending to use my inhaler as much as possible, like you said. Papa can't tell I'm only fake-inhaling, and he looks concerned. Thanks for that tip! He does seem less angry when he's worried about me.

From: Bett Devlin
To: Avery Bloom
Subject: CODE RED!!!!

I just tried to call. I think I got my period. CODE RED!

From: Avery Bloom
To: Bett Devlin
Subject: Re: CODE RED!!!!

Tried you back. No answer. Sent text. No reply. Where are you?

Do you feel sort of crampy?

Just know that it's not going to be as big a deal as you think it is once you realize that you're not actually bleeding to death.

From: Bett Devlin
To: Avery Bloom
Subject: Re: re: CODE RED!!!!

I didn't want to drag my dad into the whole thing, so I called Gaga. Right now you 2 are the ONLY ONES ON EARTH who know besides Angel, Summer, Ceci + Imani. Wait, not true. I also sent text messages to Sil + Tiana + Morgan.

Here's how it went down: So I got a weird stomach ache. Kind of like there were windscreen wipers moving deep inside me. I guess you've had this feeling before but it was new for me.

But I had eaten chicken fingers for dinner + had too

many, so I thought that was the problem. I went into the bathroom. I sat on the toilet + looked down at my underwear + there was a spot of blood there.

My first thought was "How the heck did I cut myself?" I actually stood up + looked at my legs + then I sat back down + went "Oh. Wait. Wow. Weird."

I said that out loud, like someone talking to herself in a mirror on a TV show.

I have "supplies" in the house because I'm late getting this whole thing. So I went + got a "pad". I put it in my underwear. It feels like a hot-dog bun in there. I swear to you I'm never going to get used to this! Are you used to it? Be honest. I can take the truth. I want to use a tampon, but I have to gear up for that first.

Okay, another wild thing: The DOGS know. Junie + Raisin went nuts when I (finally) came out of the bathroom.

I wish you lived closer! Please write back with tips. This is all messier than I thought it would be + definitely stranger.

Why don't people (women + girls) talk about it 24/7?

Love you.
Dogfish

From: A. Allenberry Bloom
To: Bett Devlin
Subject: Bodily functions

Dogfish –

Having your period requires a lot of planning in the beginning, but then you learn to adjust. The best thing is to keep a calendar to help remind you. I know you're not a big fan of calendars and to-do lists, but they come in handy. If you don't want to write "period" on a certain date you could just put a red dot. But maybe that would be sort of obvious. So you could put in an emoji, or draw a random picture to throw people off-track, like maybe a leprechaun.

Bookmark this new email address. It's my new secret account, and I'm only checking when I'm out of the house, which means at my friend Ariel Balakian's house. She says "hi." (Her dad is the judge, and they have the schnoodle, Sandra Day.)

Write back. I'm with Ariel all day.

xo
Love,
Night Owl

From: Bett Devlin
To: A. Allenberry Bloom
Subject: Re: Bodily functions

I swear I'll never get used to this whole PERIOD thing, but I want to believe you.

What if I get blood on a white chair? I'm going to only sit in red chairs for the next five days. I'm surprised there aren't more of them in public places.

I guess I'll try the leprechaun emoji. Also, you'll be happy to know, I'm thinking I might join the Science Club. Some of that CIGI stuff was actually kind of cool. Plus I never got to finish building my rocket + I got my maths journal back from CIGI so I started doing more calculations.

My friend Angel said they have a 3-D printer in the gifted programme. That seems pretty unfair for the rest of us, stuck in 2-D. I liked that at camp. I heard that there is a start-up in San Francisco where you can 3-D print an actual house, and then live in it.

Say "hi" to Ariel. I hope her schnoodle is good. Sandra Day isn't a good name for a dog. I would have named her Boots.

From: A. Allenberry Bloom
To: Bett Devlin
Subject: Being observed

The social worker came and "observed" me for two days last week. Once with Papa. Once with Kristina. It turns out that the hardest thing in the world to do is act natural. It's very unnatural.

During my observational visit with Kristina I could really tell she's a theatre person, because she was definitely acting. She was wearing totally different clothing than normal. Her whole outfit was all oatmeal-coloured. She looked like a zookeeper. I barely recognized her. (She didn't have on any of her regular jewellery, scarves, eyeliner, bracelets, hair extensions, or hats.)

We didn't do improv or go for Indonesian food or rearrange her furniture, like usual. Instead, we *made cookies* in front of this woman. Oatmeal cookies (maybe to match her outfit).

The whole time we were being observed Kristina never said "Brilliant!" and she didn't sing even one song. She had a calendar on the wall covered with notes that I'd never seen before. One of them said, in big letters, "Orthodontist consultation for Avery". I'm sure she made that up. You know I've got really straight teeth. There were also Post-its that said stuff like, "Check to see if Avery is taking the right vitamins". Above the sink she'd put up a sign that read: "Washing your hands is the easiest thing you can do to prevent the spread of disease".

I hope she gets a good report. She looked exhausted by the time it was over. I was exhausted too.

Love,
Avery Allenberry Bloom

From: Bett Devlin
To: A. Allenberry Bloom
Subject: Re: Being observed

I wish I could have seen Kristina in that outfit! She's a famous theatre person so I bet she was doing great improv the whole time.

All my dad does lately is work. He did that before he met your dad, but he also used to see his friends + ride his bike. Right now he's in his favourite alcove (because this place was a church, we've got a bunch of nooks) where he has his computer.

He doesn't even like to go to the gym anymore + he was kind of addicted to that place. This shows he's really messed up.

Is your dad going to the gym? Does he stare at his computer all the time with a SAD MAN LOOK?

I'm guessing your dad + my dad are sorry they got those little tattoos with their initials on their ankles.

S.B. + M.D.

My dad wears socks ALL the time now. I think the tattoo is a trigger for him. I'm never getting a tattoo with anyone else's initials. It's a mistake waiting to happen.

Gaga said I need to make Dad go places + meet new people. She said if he meets a new man he cares about it will have him smiling again. But I can't do that.

She said, "LOVE, NOT TIME, HEALS ALL WOUNDS." She got that message once in Dallas in a fortune cookie after my grandpa Alden died. She's kept it in her purse ever since.

From: A. Allenberry Bloom
To: Bett Devlin
Subject: The saddest two words

What do you think are the saddest two words in the English language?

From: Bett Devlin

To: A. Allenberry Bloom

Subject: Re: The saddest two words

    "NO PETS."

    What do YOU think?

From: A. Allenberry Bloom

To: Bett Devlin

Subject: Re: re: The saddest two words

    "If only."

2 MONTHS LATER

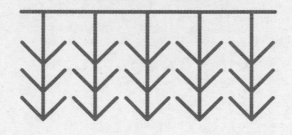

From: Bett Devlin
To: A. Allenberry Bloom
Subject: TODAY!

Happy holidays!

We just opened the stuff under our indoor lemon tree (which we decorate every year because Phillip did that). Maybe you heard me shrieking all the way in New York City. I'm not joking that my FAVOURITE PRESENT was the DOGFISH + I can't believe I sent you an OWL! We are just so in sync. We're too old for stuffed animals, but these are different.

Thank you, thank you, Avery! I also love the T-shirt with CAMP HAIR DON'T CARE. I'm going to wear it to school once the holidays are over. Also, I promise I will read *Island of the Blue Dolphins*. I see dolphins all the time + I'm glad the book is about a GIRL who is living on an island, not a lost boy or an alien.

My dad got really quiet when I was going through my stuff from you, so I said, "Christmas isn't just about opening presents, it's about opening our hearts." Angel's mom said that first. It doesn't seem like something I'd normally say, but he didn't notice.

Anyway, I looked at my dad + added, "Maybe we should Skype Avery + her papa to wish them HAPPY HOLIDAYS."

He got up from his chair + said I should just do it myself. Merry Christmas! Happy Hanukkah! Will Skype later!

Love you.
Dogfish

From: A. Allenberry Bloom
To: Bett Devlin
Subject: Re: TODAY!

It is cool that we got each other a version of the same thing. Also, isn't it amazing that we both sent each other camp T-shirts? I would wear my "Keep Calm and Camp On" T-shirt to school my first day back, but we have uniforms. It's so unfair (but it does make it easier to get organized in the morning).

I also really like the box of seagull feathers, and they do count as part of my feather collection because you found them in the wild. I appreciate that you washed them, though, because bird feathers can carry disease, but that's mostly when the feathers are on dead birds. These don't come from dead birds – right? Please confirm.

I opened the presents from my papa on the eight nights of Hanukkah. Kristina said we're going to celebrate later today. It's a good thing she and Papa agreed to a schedule, because I already know she's taking me to get my ears pierced next Tuesday.

I'm really scared it's going to hurt and also I'm concerned about infection afterwards. But I'm trying to be brave. I will only wear surgical steel post earrings, always, for the rest of my life. I've made that promise to myself.

Too bad that the Skype idea didn't work. I really think if Papa could talk to your dad about building houses (or whatever they talked about when they were so in love), maybe the magic could come back.

I was looking at Kyle Shapiro the other day and I remembered how much I liked him last year. And then just looking at him, I started liking him a little bit again. But we never went to China together. Just a school field trip to a textile museum.

Okay, happy holidays, Bett!

My wish for the New Year is going to be a secret, but I'm working on my resolution right now.

From: Bett Devlin
To: A. Allenberry Bloom
Subject: Re: re: TODAY!

I've been thinking that we should make the SAME New Year's resolution, and it should be this: WE RESOLVE TO GET OUR DADS BACK TOGETHER.

The first step is to get them in the SAME PLACE at the SAME TIME.

What do you think???

From: A. Allenberry Bloom
To: Bett Devlin
Subject: Re: re: re: TODAY!

Yes! We resolve to get these two people who can't stand each other into the same room so they can see what a mistake it was to break up in the first place, and then they can immediately fall in love again.

But how?

From: Bett Devlin
To: A. Allenberry Bloom
Subject: Re: re: re: re: TODAY!

Fortune is smiling your way. (That's on a coffee cup we have.)

I just hung up the phone with GAGA. My dad told her we're going to GO TO NEW YORK to see the opening of *HOLDING UP HALF THE SKY*, which is in only 9 weeks!

This is the break we've been looking for, Avery. Maybe your DAD could GO WITH YOU to see the play the first night? I know Kristina's not his favourite person in the world, but they did agree to a schedule for you + they aren't paying money anymore for lawyers to scare each other.

If you can't do the play, then we can arrange a fake

random meeting – like maybe that place you told me about with the frozen hot chocolate. You'd be sitting with your dad + the bell over the door would ring + you would both look up + me + my dad would be standing there.

The two dads would be like, "Whaaat???" + they would start to smile + tear up a little but pretend they weren't + you + I would go to the bathroom + let them talk in private until the miracle of deep feelings kicked in.

What do you think?

This is the greatest gift of all this Christmas. We have hope for the future as a family!

From: A. Allenberry Bloom
To: Bett Devlin
Subject Re: re: re: re: re: TODAY!

As Hamilton would say, "We are not throwing away our shot!"

You and your dad will come to New York City and we will be the welcome committee! (I didn't mean for that to rhyme. I'm not doing spoken-word poetry, I'm just excited!)

From: Bett Devlin
To: A. Allenberry Bloom
Subject: Our plan in motion

We have our plane tickets + we're going to stay at Gaga's!
Dad will sleep on the couch + I'll be in the bedroom with
Gaga, who's got a big bed. When you're staying at Kristina's,
we'll be RIGHT ACROSS THE HALL FROM EACH OTHER!

I'm glad you only LOANED the wedding books to your
cello teacher. We are probably going to need them back. I
hope she didn't fill out any of the checklists.

From: A. Allenberry Bloom
To: Bett Devlin
Subject: Possible dads meeting place: new gym

Dogfish –

My papa joined a new gym. He says it's a great place.
His New Year's resolution was to get in better shape. He's
already in good shape, but I guess there's always more to do.

He's been going to the gym a lot. Sometimes even at night.

Maybe when your dad is here, if we can't arrange for
them to see each other at the play, we could get your dad
to go to the same gym (since my papa is on a very regular

schedule). They have visitor passes, and you have to take a mandatory tour of the facilities and have your fat measured with calipers, but it doesn't take too long. I checked online.

From: Bett Devlin
To: A. Allenberry Bloom
Subject: Re: Possible dads meeting place: new gym

My dad rides his bike + he runs and he also surfs, but he doesn't go to a gym anymore. I guess I could try to get him to do that again. We only have 5 weeks left.

Why did your dad SWITCH gyms? This might be a bad sign.

He hasn't bought a lot of new clothes or anything – has he?

Also, when was the last time he got a haircut?

From: A. Allenberry Bloom
To: Bett Devlin
Subject Re: re: Possible dads meeting place: new gym

He got a haircut on Friday. And he did buy new pants last week. And new shoes. And a belt. Why? That doesn't mean anything, I don't think.

From: Bett Devlin
To: A. Allenberry Bloom
Subject: Re: re: re: Possible dads meeting place: new gym

Let me know if you see him doing CRUNCHES at night. After my dad met your dad, he started doing A LOT of crunches.

Also, check his toothpaste. If he switches to something that's got more TEETH WHITENER, we're in a bad place.

My dad's still staring out the window + eating a lot of breakfast cereal at weird hours, so he's good to go.

From: A. Allenberry Bloom
To: Bett Devlin
Subject: B-O-B

Dogfish,

You were right. No one gets a haircut or starts buying new clothes without a reason. It gives me waves of nausea to even type this, but we now have the reason. And the reason has a name:

Bob

I can't believe my papa could ever fall for a Bob. But five minutes ago I asked him if there was someone new romantically in his life, and he had this sort of shy smile and admitted that there is a Man-Named-Bob in the picture.

From: Bett Devlin
To: A. Allenberry Bloom
Subject: A Man Named B-O-B

I KNEW IT.

This is a real setback. With SUCH BAD TIMING. We are so close to the dads finally being in the same room again since they broke up + suddenly realizing it was a big mistake + that they are still in love.

Also, BOB is a very old-school name + super boring.

How serious are they? Are you going to MEET HIM?

Is it THAT advanced?

From: A. Allenberry Bloom
To: Bett Devlin
Subject: Re: A Man Named B-O-B

Papa just came in while I was typing (he doesn't know it was to you) and said that Bob is coming over on Saturday.

He explained they've been going out for three and a half weeks. Doesn't this mean he's counting the days?

So far all I really know is that his name is a palindrome (it's spelled the same way backwards and forwards). "Palindrome" is often on standardized vocabulary tests, but it's a weird word that people never say out loud, which is probably why those tests are unfair.

I really like palindromes, but Bob should change his name to Otto if he wants to be more interesting.

For now he's *Bob Bilderback*.

Only I would never dislike someone just because they had an awkward name. His parents were Bilderbacks, so it's not his fault.

But I don't like him for other reasons.

From: Bett Devlin
To: A. Allenberry Bloom
Subject: Re: re: A Man Named B-O-B

When you meet Bob, try to be AWFUL, but in LOTS OF SMALL WAYS. That's usually better than one big bad thing.

That SNIFFING you do that you say is from sensitivity to humidity is super annoying. You could start with that.

Also, he doesn't have any kids of his own – right?

From: A. Allenberry Bloom
To: Bett Devlin
Subject: Re: re: re: A Man Named B-O-B

My first question to Papa was whether Bob Bilderback had children!

No, Bob has no kids. He's just coming out of a long-term relationship (too bad we can't find *that* guy and get some dirt on the Palindrome).

I can't take any more drama. Two days ago Kristina asked Papa if she could move her night from Monday to Tuesday (just this once) and Papa acted like she'd asked him to donate an organ. I guess he and B-O-B had already made plans for Monday.

When I went to Kristina's she got takeout and we watched a very old movie (not black-and-white) called *KRAMER VS KRAMER*. Kristina cried before it was even sad, so she knew the story already. (Parents fight over custody of their kid.) I guess we're living it.

Gaga was going to come across the hall to Kristina's apartment and watch with us, but she wanted to try out a new Jazz Dance class. She says it's important to build stamina before the opening of the play.

From: Bett Devlin
To: A. Allenberry Bloom
Subject: Re: re: re: re: A Man Named B-O-B

My friend Angel has divorced parents + for a while they were doing the weekly "hand-off" (that's what they call it) in the police station parking lot, which was super awkward. But my friend Zoe also has divorced parents + they all go on holiday to Hawaii together + stay in the same condo.

So there's lots of ways to do it. Some are just way easier on kids.

Tell Kristina I can't WAIT to see her. And report back Saturday on Bob Bilderback. But remember one word: SABOTAGE.

That would be a good name for a pet HAWK.

Is it legal to own a hawk?

From: A. Allenberry Bloom
To: Bett Devlin
Subject: Re: re: re: re: re: A Man Named B-O-B

I know people keep falcons, so maybe they keep hawks.

I could see you training to be a falconer one day, but I don't think you'd like that the birds need to catch and eat live rabbits and squirrels and must hunt them down while the falcon-owner stands by and watches, wearing a leather glove that goes to their elbow.

I guess you could close your eyes during all of this, but it still sounds traumatic. I know this because I went to the Renaissance Faire in Tuxedo, New York, once with my papa. People were eating those smoked turkey drumsticks that are the size of caveman clubs.

If he went today he'd probably just take Bob. And my papa wouldn't eat a drumstick, but he and Bob would take turns drinking mead from the same giant silver cup. Ugh.

From: Bett Devlin
To: A. Allenberry Bloom
Subject: Re: re: re: re: re: re: A Man Named B-O-B

I'm not going to get a hawk as a pet. Or be a falconer. All birds should be free.

From: A. Allenberry Bloom
To: Bett Devlin
Subject: Re: re: re: re: re: re: re: A Man Named B-O-B

All kids, too.

From: A. Allenberry Bloom

To: Bett Devlin

Subject: Re: re: re: re: re: re: re: re: A Man Named B-O-B

Bob just left. What a phony. When Papa brought him into the den, he acted as if he'd stumbled upon me accidentally, not that he'd come to the apartment just to meet me. He looked over with fake-surprise and said, "Well, *who* do we have *here*?"

I wanted to say, "An angry girl with seasonal allergies who wants you to leave *right now*." But I didn't. I smiled (but my eyes were as dull as I could make them, which really means just not blinking).

He'd been fully prepped, but he still talked to me like I was five years old. He bent down and in this singsong voice he said, "So tell me about yourself, Avery. What's something you collect?"

Why would someone *just assume* a kid collected stuff? It's really insulting.

Okay, I do have my organic material scarves and my first edition novels, and also my minor obsession with feathers (found in the wild only, as you know). There's also *National Geographic* magazines dated from before 1962 (and in excellent condition). But that's all *none of his business*.

So I just said, "Nothing."

After he was gone (which took a while) I asked Papa, "No offence, but does Bob seem sort of *off* to you?"

To which he said, "He has no experience with children. He lives in his own world." Then Papa actually laughed, as if living in your own world is a great thing.

Here is what else I learned while pretending to be doing a science project but actually listening while Papa and the Palindrome sat talking and sipping double espressos and eating maybe seven almonds: Bob is a lawyer. But supposedly the good kind, fighting justice. (I mean, injustice.) He's thirty-six years old and works out at the Michael Scanlon gym every morning at 6:00 a.m. for ninety minutes (that's Papa's new gym) before using a Citi Bike to go 4.8 miles to his office. That level of exercise seems excessive. He might have 8 per cent measurable body fat. I'm not sure I heard correctly.

I think one of the main things my papa likes about Bob is that he believes that this kind of person would never want to ride a motorcycle across China. Which is probably true.

I'm afraid Bob will be in charge of their whole relationship, because Papa's in a still-wounded state.

I heard him tell Bob, "Well, I already have a kid. That's been the best thing by far to ever happen to me. But no, I wouldn't rule out another one."

It's possible my heart actually stopped.

Since Bob left I've had to use my inhaler three times. For real.

From: Bett Devlin
To: A. Allenberry Bloom
Subject: Collections

Why would anyone think that just because you're a KID you COLLECT stuff? That's so wrong + also so insulting + a stereotype.

I collect:

Little DOG figures
Little SHARK figures
SHELLS (they don't have to be found by me, I've bought some good ones at garage sales)
ORANGE T-shirts with sayings on the front
Pictures of MEERKATS

Question: Maybe we should start a collection TOGETHER? We would have West Coast + East Coast versions of things.

From: A. Allenberry Bloom
To: Bett Devlin
Subject: Re: Collections

I think this is a great idea.

But we don't want to collect trading cards. Or erasers or perfume bottles. Obviously.

From: Bett Devlin
To: A. Allenberry Bloom
Subject: Re: re: Collections

OBVIOUSLY is right.

I'd like to collect small water animals (live), but that's not going to happen. On top of all the other problems, they would be hard to share back and forth.

Maybe we can start with key chains.

From: A. Allenberry Bloom
To: Bett Devlin
Subject: Re: re: re: Collections

Key chains are a good start. There is a key chain in the drawer in the kitchen. It's shaped like a crow. I don't know where it came from. Maybe that should be the first thing in our collection.

From: Bett Devlin
To: A. Allenberry Bloom
Subject: Re: re: re: re: Collections

There is a difference between crows and ravens. Did you know this?

Please confirm which bird is on the key chain.

From: A. Allenberry Bloom
To: Bett Devlin
Subject: Re: re: re: re: re: Collections

I wasn't aware of this bird difference but now I will read up. I guess there were a lot of crows and maybe ravens in NYC once, but they got sick and mostly died. Pigeons inherited the place. We get a lot of bird droppings on our window ledge and have to clean it off, but only wearing rubber gloves, for hygiene.

People are always saying crows are so smart. (Not as smart as owls, of course!) I wonder why exactly?

From: Bett Devlin
To: A. Allenberry Bloom
Subject: Re: re: re: re: re: re: Collections

At CIGI you should have done an experiment with a crow instead of on J.K. Rowling the chicken + we might have the answer. Do people eat crow eggs? Does a bird have to cluck before you can eat one of the eggs?

I'm just thinking out loud here.

From: A. Allenberry Bloom
To: Bett Devlin
Subject: Re: re: re: re: re: re: re: Collections

You're always thinking out loud, Dogfish. That's one of the things I like about you.

From: Bett Devlin
To: A. Allenberry Bloom
Subject: Re: re: re: re: re: re: re: re: Collections

Thanks! You can tell a crow's AGE by the COLOUR of its eyes. BABY CROWS have BROWN in the centre. When they get older, the brown turns to WHITE. At some point they have BLUE eyes, but I can't remember when.

We have crows everywhere in California. But it's hard to get CLOSE enough to see their EYEBALLS.

Next time you see BOB, ask him if he knows the DIFFERENCE between these birds. This will tell us if Bob watches *Animal Planet*. I'm betting he doesn't.

From: A. Allenberry Bloom
To: Bett Devlin
Subject: Re: re: re: re: re: re: re: re: re: Collections

I'm hoping right now that there isn't a "next time I see Bob".

From: Bett Devlin
To: A. Allenberry Bloom
Subject: Re: re: re: re: re: re: re: re: re: re: Collections

Same.

From: A. Allenberry Bloom
To: Bett Devlin
Subject: Re: re: re: re: re: re: re: re: re: re: re: Collections

Only sixteen days until your trip to NY. Of course I've got a calendar alert set!

Are you having second thoughts on the key chains?

I'm thinking that pressed flowers might be better. What do you think? We could send them back and forth in books.

From: Bett Devlin
To: A. Allenberry Bloom
Subject: Re: re: re: re: re: re: re: re: re: re: re: re: Collections

So would our collection be BOOKS or PRESSED FLOWERS? I feel like this might be a way to trick me into joining your reading club.

I'm not falling for that, Night Owl.

From: A. Allenberry Bloom

To: Bett Devlin

Subject: Re: re: re: re: re: re: re: re: re: re: re: re: re: Collections

Ha! I swear to you I wasn't tricking you, Dogfish.

From: Bett Devlin

To: A. Allenberry Bloom

Subject: Re: re: re: re: re: re: re: re: re: re: re: re: re: re: Collections

K. I believe you. I think.

From: A. Allenberry Bloom

To: Bett Devlin

Subject: Re: re: re: re: re: re: re: re: re: re: re: re: re: re: Collections

I've been reading about the pressed flowers. It's actually considered a craft. That's different from a collection. Maybe it's even better!

I just discovered that Emily Dickinson (the famous poet) probably had agoraphobia, because it doesn't sound like she left her yard very much. She had what's called a "herbarium", which is a collection of pressed plants in an album. She did this when she was only fourteen years old. And she ended up with four hundred different specimens!

This project would have made a great college application essay for her, but I don't know if they had that back in her time.

From: Bett Devlin
To: A. Allenberry Bloom
Subject: Re: re: re: re: re: re: re: re: re: re: re: re: re: re: re: re: Collections

So are we pressing PLANTS or FLOWERS?

From: A. Allenberry Bloom
To: Bett Devlin
Subject: Re: re: re: re: re: re: re: re: re: re: re: re: re: re: re: re: Collections

You know what we are? Flower girls.

From: Bett Devlin
To: A. Allenberry Bloom
Subject: Flower Girls

Flower Girls. Cool. FGs.

I was just thinking that it would be interesting to press a tree (small) but also very hard + then I thought, wait, isn't that what paper is?

I'm trying to press some dandelions. The problem is that I keep lifting up the books to check on the progress. It's very messy.

Here's another thing that's messy. I asked my dad if he was going to CALL YOUR DAD while we were on our NYC trip, even to say hi. He said, "No, Bett, I'm not. You know that. That relationship is over + in the past now. So please STOP."

What a bad attitude! But he has been doing a lot of yoga, so I said, "Dad, are you taking yoga classes because it's relaxing you + that's helping you get over Sam?"

He got all mad + said, "Of course not. I've been over Sam for months now."

So that means FOR SURE it's why he's doing yoga!

WHEN are you going to see if YOUR DAD WILL GO WITH YOU to the play on opening night?

From: A. Allenberry Bloom
To: Bett Devlin
Subject: Re: Flower Girls

I'm still waiting for the right time to ask. But if I can't make him go to the opening night it's going to be work for us to get them to "accidentally" bump into each other on the street, even with mobile phones and the world of technology and all of our planning, which could include a frozen hot chocolate meeting.

Right now I'm pressing a crocus.

It's challenging.

From: Bett Devlin
To: A. Allenberry Bloom
Subject: Re: re: Flower Girls

I think that BOB can now be USED to help us. Maybe you could say you WANT Bob to get to know your mom's work. That might lead your dad to believe you're INTO the idea of Bob.

Maybe then he would go to the play?

I'll try to come up with other ideas if this one seems bad to you.

FYI. I added a second dandelion, which is what's called a blowball. It's the big white cluster with the seeds. It's doing WAY better than the yellow dandelion flower.

From: A. Allenberry Bloom
To: Bett Devlin
Subject: Final plan

I can't sleep. It's not my usual insomnia brought on by worrying about things like climate change or flesh-eating bacteria. (Both on the rise.) I don't think about that stuff as much anymore at night. It started to get a little repetitive.

I can't sleep because things are really heating up with Papa and the Palindrome. They went out last night at *midnight* for dumplings.

Only people who are getting serious do those kinds of things, because it means one person has a craving and the other person gives in to that.

I didn't know a dandelion seed head was called a blowball. But that makes sense.

From: Bett Devlin
To: A. Allenberry Bloom
Subject: Re: Final plan

THAT'S SUPER-BAD NEWS about Bob + the midnight dumplings. But you are lucky you live close to a place that stays open that late. I really love pan-fried dumplings (better than steamed, which can be mushy).

I had a new idea. What about using your BIRTHDAY (coming up!) to get your dad to the play. Make it a birthday WISH that you could go together. You could just casually say, "You know what I'd like, Papa? If you + I could go see Kristina's play together. It would mean a lot as I turn thirteen + become a teenager. Also, that might be a fun thing for us to do with Bob."

Our dads last saw each other when they were at the airport in China, still getting over their lost passports. This is a very bad association memory. No wonder they broke up.

xo
Dogfish

P.S. Fun fact that Angel told me: The French words *dent de lion* are why the weeds are called dandelions. She said it means "tooth of a lion". Angel's very into where words come from. You'd like her.

From: Betty Devlin
To: Bett Devlin
Subject: You're almost here

I'm just rotating in my shell waiting for you! Who would have thought that I'd be living in New York City and starring in a play?

Here's what my days are now like. I haul myself out of bed and take the elevator downstairs. I get my coffee with Dinos. He brews a pot for the workers, but he doesn't mind if I head back into the mail area and help myself to a big cup. Dinos is the morning doorman. The doormen are in a union. Not a union like they're a couple, but the worker kind. Your grandpa would've loved to see it. He was a union man to the core.

I made my famous peanut brittle last week and Dinos was the first person to get some. He's from Greece and just the sweetest. But he chipped a crown on his second bite! We're still friends because he's got great dental insurance. After we chew the fat (and sort the mail) I go back upstairs and take out my curlers. Once I've got my hair done up it's almost rehearsal time.

Once a week our Avery comes to visit Kristina. Since she's right across the hall she always stops in. Last time she brought over a locket and put a picture of herself on one side and you on the other. That sweet girl gave it to me, and I'm proud to say I haven't taken it off even though my hair gets all twisted on the clasp.

Okay! I'm counting the days till we're together. Hugs and bugs!

Your Gaga

From: A. Allenberry Bloom
To: Bett Devlin
Subject: Victory

It's done. Papa asked what I want to do for my birthday, and I told him I'd like him to go with me to see the opening of Kristina's play. I put on a faraway, dreamy face to make it seem like it was something impossible.

At first he said, "No. I can't. I'm not going to give a public show of support to Kristina."

I answered, "You'd be going to support *me*."

It was a great response because he just stopped talking.

Then I brought in the final thing. I managed to get tears in my eyes (mostly because I was thinking about how Bob was making this *a lot harder* for you and me), and in a really quiet, kind of younger version of my voice I said, "I was hoping you'd ask Bob to come with us."

Papa looked surprised. I ended with, "If you and Bob want to go with me, Kristina would like to give us seats. Orchestra. Right in the centre."

He said he'd think about it. But he went down the hall and I heard him making a phone call.

It was to Bob. And he said, "Hey, you. Want to go to a play?"

From: Bett Devlin
To: A. Allenberry Bloom
Subject: A Fake Date

BEST NEWS EVER! I told Gaga that on opening night our dads will see each other + after all this time apart it will be a positive trigger for both of them.

Gaga said, "I just hope one of them doesn't PULL A TRIGGER on the other!"

She was just being Gaga because of course we are all for gun control.

So then I said your dad was bringing a guy named BOB BILDERBACK to the play + we were worried Bob would hurt our chances for the trigger moment between our dads, but it was a risk we had to take.

Gaga hung up + went across the hall to Kristina's. She called me back 20 minutes later to say that Kristina has a great idea. She thinks that my dad should ALSO LOOK LIKE HE'S WITH SOMEONE ON OPENING NIGHT of the play! So she's going to get another ticket + make sure to get a great guy sitting in that seat.

She said that there's one thing she knows about your dad: "He's a competitor + a jealous man."

Do you think that's true?

Kristina says YOUR dad will flip out when he sees MY dad next to this AMAZING GUY. I don't know his name yet, but the person she's thinking about is from Cuba + he's a dancer + everyone in the theatre world is talking about him. He hasn't been in America that long, but he's really good at English, and besides, MY DAD speaks Spanish.

Also, Kristina says that there is a PARTY after the opening night show + that we should try to get the DADS + THE DECOYS there.

There is only one problem now. HOW do we tell my dad that he has a FAKE DATE to the play?

Let me know if you have any ideas. I'm hoping to get them to hold hands, since if your dad is really competitive + a jealous man that could totally set things in motion.

I'm pressing a wildflower that has a star in the middle + I was remembering how we had to learn to DRAW A STAR when we were little but not lift the pencil. Did you have to learn to do that?

I wish we did stuff like that now. Those were the days.

From: A. Allenberry Bloom
To: Bett Devlin
Subject: Javier

Kristina is really coming through for us! The fake date said yes! His name is Javier Martinez and he said he's up for the adventure, just as long as he can be on his own at the after-party. But before that he promises to be very into your dad. How awesome is this guy?

My dad is going to be so jealous. Bob will be so boring compared to Javier, but more to the point, compared to your dad.

Maybe one day we will tell them we were the match-makers. We could even reveal it during the toasts at their wedding.

Lots of love from your (hopefully) future sister,
xo
Night Owl

P.S. Working on pressing a tulip. Degree of difficulty = 10. And yes, we also had to learn to do the star without lifting the pencil. I think it's to teach coordination. Or maybe to give the teachers some time to themselves.

From: Bett Devlin
To: A. Allenberry Bloom
Subject: Re: Javier

Javier Martinez is an AMAZING secret weapon to get our dads back together. I read about him. He's a big deal dancer for the BALLET HISPÁNICO.

His bio says that he grew up in Cuba without toys. But he loved all kinds of sports + swam in the ocean every day (not fun for you, but for most people). His mom put him in a ballet programme one summer, only really it was because they served hot lunch.

Javier knows Kristina because they might do a project together. Also, he's met Gaga. He came over to the apartment. She speaks Spanish + I guess they had a fun time.

Can you believe how this is all going so GREAT?

Except for Bob Bilderback existing + also our dads not liking each other anymore.

I tried to press a water lily. Bad idea. Do not attempt. I stuck it in a book. Good thing I'd already read it + wasn't a big fan. (Dystopian + really depressing. Who needs it?)

From: A. Allenberry Bloom
To: Bett Devlin
Subject: Re: re: Javier

Yes, Javier Martinez is a great guy to be sitting next to your dad at the play. Everyone will notice him since he's like a statue come to life, and his man-bun is very cool.

I had a thought: What if Bob Bilderback falls for the Cuban dancer?

Two birds, one stone!

That's such a violent expression. I mean, who throws rocks at birds? And the idea of using one rock to take down two birds is just horrifying. But I'm guessing the stone was fired in a slingshot in medieval times.

We're so lucky we live now, and not just because of the advancements in the medical field, but because who wants to carry around a slingshot? Also, we have better hygiene now.

From: Bett Devlin
To: A. Allenberry Bloom
Subject: Re: re: re: Javier

Hygiene issues in olden times were probably horrible. What did women do each month when they got their *"leprechaun"*? Did they have to use hay?

Also, when were tampons even invented?

What did they do for the zillion years before that?

From: A. Allenberry Bloom
To: Bett Devlin
Subject: Medieval hygiene and healthcare

I just read online that in medieval times, guess what women used instead of pads or tampons?

Moss. I'm writing this twice because you probably don't believe it: moss.

I don't even understand how that would work. And how do they know these things? Did people "journal" about their monthly moss usage?

I feel totally ill now thinking about it.

From: Bett Devlin
To: A. Allenberry Bloom
Subject: Re: Medieval hygiene and healthcare

The moss is a horrible fact to know. I will never sit on a mossy hill the same way.

All of this has me thinking: I know that my dad + your dad had a FAVOURITE SONG when they were together + that it was "IT'S OUR TIME" by the Eye Sockets.

I'll try to learn to play it on the recorder (only when Dad's not home). See if you can learn it on your cello. We may need to break into song at some point to help with the mood.

See you soon, under a New York moon.

From: A. Allenberry Bloom
To: Bett Devlin
Subject: It's our time

I think it's better if we *sing* their song. We don't have a lot of flexibility with the recorder and the cello. It means we would have to be dragging around the instruments and that's not very practical in the city. If we just sang

"It's Our Time" at the right moment in two-part harmony that could be very effective.

Can you sing like an angel? By that I just mean soprano. I know you said you don't have the greatest singing voice, but it's really about getting the words right. I'll carry the tune.

From: Bett Devlin
To: A. Allenberry Bloom
Subject: Re: It's our time

Dad got a haircut today + he did some crunches!

This means he wants to look his best for the New York trip, which is a VERY GOOD SIGN.

Final question: When exactly are you thinking we sing the song? I mean, IF we sing it.

Okay, that's it for now. See you in only 3 days!

Yours in crime,
Dogfish

From: Kristina Allenberry
To: Javier Martinez
Subject: Tomorrow night

Excited for tomorrow. You never know how a performance will go, but I've got a good feeling.

It will be the first time experiencing a NY opening with my daughter. And having Bett (Gaga's granddaughter) and you there, too, will be awesome. I'm hoping Sam stays under control. He now has Bob.

The girls are so desperate for Sam and Marlow to give it another chance. I'm not saying I have any idea how that would even work, but at least with you there the maths is balanced. I owe you, Javier.

Con besos,
Kristina

P.S. Here's Marlow's info if you want to get in touch first. Up to you.

From: Javier Martinez
To: D. Marlow Devlin
Subject: Theatre Night in NYC

Marlow –

I want to introduce myself before we meet. I'm
Kristina's friend and we're all going to the theatre together
tomorrow night.

Dance is my first language. Spanish is my second
language. English is my third language.

Es verdad que hablas español?

I met your mother and her Spanish was great! So was
she!

All the best,
Javier

From: A. Allenberry Bloom
To: Bett Devlin
Subject: Re: re: It's our time

I can now play the song on the cello (even though the
plan is still to just do the singing). But if we all do end up
back here at our apartment (and there's a big chance of

that) then I'll play the cello. So bring your recorder.

Also, I don't know much about aromatherapy, but are there some candles or scented oils that we should consider? Smells can stir up memories, and maybe our dads would respond (and not even realize it at first).

From: Bett Devlin
To: A. Allenberry Bloom
Subject: Re: re: re: It's our time

I'm at the airport right now with my dad. Don't get mad, but I forgot the recorder + the scented candles. I bet Kristina has a whole drawer full. Could you check? We almost missed our plane because of a traffic problem, but the flight was delayed! So it really was OUR TIME. HA!

I'm GETTING OUT OF A DAY OF SCHOOL for this. There's nothing better. But I have to write a report on the play for Mrs Wetterling. She's secretly a theatre person.

We sent Gaga flowers today to say congratulations. We picked sunflowers because those are her favourite. I bet it's hard to press a sunflower.

I'll see you tonight in row F!

From: A. Allenberry Bloom
To: Bett Devlin
Subject: Row F

Remember to act surprised when we're seated next to each other. I'll probably squeal a little.

I'm going to have my phone, and I could record my papa's face (which might not be too excited when he *first* sees your dad, but *will be* excited as the night goes on). That footage would be fun to show at their wedding rehearsal dinner!

Gaga says that the first night you're staying at her place but the next night you're staying with me at Kristina's. If things work out maybe on the last night you can come stay with me at Papa's!

THE VERY NEXT DAY

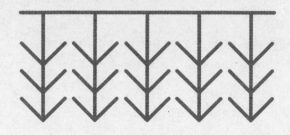

From: Bett Devlin
To: A. Allenberry Bloom
Subject: I just woke up

It's 7:00 a.m. + I have DISTURBING NEWS. Gaga is still asleep. I'm not going to go into how great the play was or how much fun it was to see you, because WE HAVE A BIG PROBLEM.

Very awkward, but MY DAD IS HERE + SO IS JAVIER.

I guess they've been up talking all night long.

You read that right. Dad went with Javier for a drink AFTER the party after the play, which had all kinds of drinks so they were definitely NOT thirsty. They just wanted to spend more time together.

Gaga fell asleep + I stayed up waiting for Dad. It got so late that I started to wonder if he fell on to the subway tracks + was electrocuted by the third rail or was kidnapped by an Uber driver. You told me both of those things can happen in New York. But then I saw a text on Gaga's phone that said:

I'M WITH JAVIER WALKING THE STREETS OF THIS AMAZING CITY. EVERYTHING IS FANTASTIC! HOME SOON!

After that is a thumbs-up.

So I went to sleep, hoping it was all nothing. But I just woke up + I can hear them in the living room + they can't stop laughing.

What have we DONE? I mean, I liked Javier but this was NOT THE PLAN!

Your dad was supposed to get JEALOUS!

Do you think he got jealous? He didn't look jealous.

BOB looked more interested in my dad + Javier than your dad, who kept staring at his phone. Was he checking sports scores? He was scrolling through a lot of things.

Please come GET ME as soon as possible. I need pancakes. This is a PANCAKE EMERGENCY. Do you think Kristina has any Bisquick mix? Probably not. But I bet Gaga does.

Okay, REALLY waiting to hear from you.

xo
Dogfish in 12B

From: A. Allenberry Bloom
To: Bett Devlin
Subject: Disturbing news

I'm awake. I'm coming over right now. I'm not even looking for the pancake mix.

From: Javier Martinez
To: Kristina Allenberry
Subject: *GRACIAS*

I LOVE the play. I know the reviews will be amazing because the work is amazing. Betty (Gaga!) is the best. You said that a lot of that dialogue came straight from her. I don't know if she's acting or being herself, but either way she's going to be a star.

Here's another thing I want to say about last night: Right when I met Marlow I felt a kind of magic. We went from the party to the after-party and then back to the apartment, and we talked until the moon got lost in the river and the sun came up. Call it love at first sight?

But now what do I do? Move to California? And take the Ballet Hispánico company with me?

Besos,
Javi

From: Betty Devlin
To: Bett Devlin
Subject: Plans are changing

Bett honey,

Javier left to go home to Brooklyn and your daddy's thinking of heading out there, too. He wants you to go with him but he says you're not answering his calls or texts.

I feel like I got hit with a sledgehammer. Too much celebrating. Dinos the doorman brought me up a cup of coffee. Good thing, or I'd be back asleep for two days. And I've got a show to do tonight.

It meant so much to have you there last night, Bett. I'm keeping your flowers in my dressing room. Maybe you and Avery want to try and press one? The memories I have from last night will last forever.

From: Bett Devlin
To: Betty Devlin
Subject: Pollo con arroz y frijoles

I'm with Dad in Brooklyn at Javier's. They're cooking *pollo con arroz y frijoles*. The place smells really good.

Gaga, I only saw part of the play when we were at

Seelocken, so it was fun to watch the whole thing. I'm not sure I understand it all but I can see it again when I'm older + it will make more sense. I think. But you were amazing. That much is for real.

I'm having fun, but nothing is going like Avery + I planned.

We thought BOB was going to mess stuff up. But it turns out that TROUBLE has a new name: JAVIER.

From: A. Allenberry Bloom
To: Bett Devlin
Subject: Everybody but us

Kristina is really happy because of the reviews.

Gaga is really happy eating something called baklava with the doorman downstairs.

Your dad is really happy hanging out in Brooklyn with Javier.

I guess my papa and Bob are really happy somewhere.

And then there's us.

From: Bett Devlin
To: A. Allenberry Bloom
Subject: Re: Everybody but us

I'll tell you one thing. We don't need to rehearse "It's Our Time".

From: Sam Bloom
To: Marlow Devlin
Subject: Coffee?

Marlow, I had no idea you would be at the play. The girls obviously planned the whole thing, since we were all in the same row. Hope that wasn't too awkward for you. I'm going to confess it was awkward for me, though seeing Bett and Avery together was really something. Their bond is totally obvious. They came out of the bathroom at the interval dancing.

I'm not proud of some of my behaviour when it comes to the two of us. I hadn't been in a real relationship in a long time when we met in Chicago at the Building Expo. What I wanted to tell you last night, but didn't get a chance, was that I'm sorry. And in that spirit of explanation, I want to tell you that I got an email from Shanghai last week. They found my leather bag. It was in a ditch on the side of one of the roads to Xinjiang. Everything was still in it.

So I guess that means you didn't leave it in the hotel after all. The bag fell off the back of the motorcycle. We both packed that morning, so in the end we were both to blame.

Maybe you and I (without the kids) could get coffee before you head back home to California?

Sam

P.S. Your mother was incredible onstage!

From: Marlow Devlin
To: Sam Bloom
Subject: Re: Coffee

Yes, I guess our girls were excited to see each other, and for us to be together as well. You're right, they were behind it all. They're really a force, those two.

I appreciate your apology. I'm sorry as well. But good news about the bag – right? Even if it's so long after our trip. So now that we've got that out of the way, you looked happy with Bob at the play. I've found someone else, too. It happened really fast, and I'm not going to make myself nuts forming fantasies about the future (okay, I admit, I'm already figuring out how to make two lives work as one. You know the drill – we did that).

Sam, you opened up my heart, and I'm hoping the mistakes I made with you won't be repeated. Thank God we each have our girls – right? Bett is the one thing in my life that is pure joy. And even though I change my password every week, she somehow cracks the code. So if you're reading this, my darling girl, STOP RIGHT NOW.

I wish getting coffee would work, but I'm going to have to take a rain check because every minute is spoken for.

Marlow

From: Bett Devlin
To: A. Allenberry Bloom
Subject: Re: re: Everybody but us

Javier doesn't have TV + I forgot to bring my book so I'm just sitting here in Brooklyn with my phone + I'm thinking about Kristina's play.

When Gaga came out onstage + started crying + said that women have different choices to make in their lives, my dad reached over + took my hand.

What did you think when that tall actor, playing a gay guy, yelled at that short lady carrying a picket sign, "I will HAVE a family or NOT have a family. It's up to me!"?

Gay people having families doesn't seem like something anyone should have to shout about anymore. Some people are a lot more interested in raising kids than other people. From what I can see, the person most interested usually does the best job.

I probably want to have a family someday.

But I also want to raise a capybara. They are the largest rodents in the world (but SUPER CUTE) + can weigh up to 140 pounds, so if you wanted to take one anywhere it would be like carrying around a person, unless you could get them used to a lead. But I'm not sure that's how capybaras roll.

From: A. Allenberry Bloom
To: Bett Devlin
Subject: Re: re: re: Everybody but us

Kristina was talking to me about the play and she explained that most artists work on something that "animates their soul". She said she means we all have things we care about in a big way. Or at least we should.

She asked me what animates my soul and I didn't have an answer.

I'm not sure I want to be a writer anymore (don't tell Kristina or Gaga that I said that). I might want to go into stem cell research. I was interested in that before CIGI, so the camp doesn't get the credit.

I think medical facts animate my soul. Because I'm afraid of diseases, I've learned a lot. It can be scary but also very interesting.

A

From: Bett Devlin
To: A. Allenberry Bloom
Subject: Re: re: re: re: Everybody but us

What animates my soul is having a friend like you. We're so different, but we're the same in the ways that matter. Mrs. Maynard, who teaches PE, gave us a quote to think about when we're going through something hard.

It was "Someday EVEN THIS will be a good memory".

A guy named Virgil wrote it. I guess a lot of people think he was a white guy, but Mrs. Maynard said that he might have been a person of colour. He wrote those words a long time ago + they still read his stuff today.

Maybe you'll be a doctor + I'll be a writer. I'd probably write books about animals + kids. When you think about it, doctors + writers aren't that different.

Both of them have to care about living things in order to be any good at their job.

From: A. Allenberry Bloom
To: Bett Devlin
Subject: Someday EVEN THIS will be a good memory

Thanks.

And it's the same for me. The idea of you as my sister animates my soul.

From: Bett Devlin
To: A. Allenberry Bloom
Subject: Re: Someday EVEN THIS will be a good memory

Also night owls + dogfish + puppies + hummingbirds + raccoons + pigs named Wilbur + Minnie + a chicken named J.K. Rowling + any animal in need of help.

From: A. Allenberry Bloom
To: Bett Devlin
Subject: Re: re: Someday EVEN THIS will be a good memory

Especially any animal in need of help.

From: Bett Devlin
To: A. Allenberry Bloom
Subject: Re: re: re: Someday EVEN THIS will be a good memory

MOST especially.

From: A. Allenberry Bloom
To: Bett Devlin
Subject: A tangled web

I'm hoping you get Wi-Fi on the plane and can read this.

After you and your dad left Gaga's, my papa picked me up. We went home for dinner and talked about the play, which he said was interesting. He won't say "good" – that would be too much of a compliment – but he did say that Gaga was great. Then he brought up Bob Bilderback and said that he's such a solid guy, only maybe he's *too* solid.

He was saying Bob was a stump.

I wanted to leap up and shout: "You got *that* right!" but I didn't, because then the worst part happened. Papa started to cry. It made me feel so bad that I started to cry, too. I was crying because he was crying, but he thought I was crying about Bob Bilderback.

Papa said, "You really like Bob – am I right?"

I got out, through my tears, "No! I don't like Bob. I mean, I *really* don't."

Then Papa started to laugh. He was crying, but he was also laughing.

It was totally great.

I think this means Bob is out of the picture (but might not know it yet).

Now we just have to get rid of Javier, the most amazing ballet dancer in the world. Who I guess is also a cook with a great sense of humour and a cool rooftop apartment in Brooklyn.

But we have no one to be mad at except ourselves. Gaga said we were the ones who were setting the honey trap. Fingers crossed that what's happening now is some kind of love-at-first-sight crush, and your dad and Javier the ballet dancer get over it very quickly.

And we can get back to the business of making our dads fall in love again.

Message me when you're home with any updates. I'm seeing Kristina and Gaga twice this week. Papa has suddenly eased up on the schedule. Not sure what any of it means, but as Gaga would say, "Winner Winner Chicken Dinner!"

And I don't even eat chicken.

From: Bett Devlin
To: A. Allenberry Bloom
Subject: Re: A tangled web

Thanks to us, your dad ditched Bob + is now in the right place. Only my dad is in the wrong place. He's suddenly some kind of ballet SUPER FAN. On the plane he signed up online for BEGINNING BALLET CLASS at a dance studio in Culver City. That means crossing the 405 freeway. No one crosses the 405 freeway for fun.

From: A. Allenberry Bloom
To: Bett Devlin
Subject: Re: re: A tangled web

Your dad is signed up for ballet. My papa is now going to take a Spanish class. I think learning a new skill is good, but is this all because of Javier?

My papa *really* is a jealous and competitive man. I guess he couldn't stand seeing your dad and Javier speaking Spanish together. He took French in college.

There was a study that said that people who suffer from chronic daily headaches get amazing relief when they fall in love. It's because of the chemical that's released, which is called oxytocin.

I'm guessing your dad doesn't have a headache right now. But we do.

2 MONTHS LATER

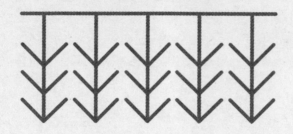

From: Bett Devlin
To: A. Allenberry Bloom
Subject: Dead centre

Dad + Javier are meeting in Oklahoma. It's DEAD CENTRE in the middle of the country. We have to hope they have a horrible time.

I once thought you + me + our dads might live there someday as a family + we'd get tickets to the Oklahoma Thunder + hunt for dinosaur bones on the weekends. They have them there for real.

From: A. Allenberry Bloom
To: Bett Devlin
Subject: Re: Dead Centre

Oklahoma? I just looked and the state bird is a scissor-tailed flycatcher. The state flower is a rose. You could ask your dad to bring one back so you could try and press it, but on second thought we don't want negative memories to be part of our collection.

From: Bett Devlin
To: A. Allenberry Bloom
Subject: Re: re: Dead centre

I didn't ask for the Oklahoma rose. He brought back a little stuffed-animal buffalo. He told me Javier picked it out. I put it on my bed + about an hour later Junie ripped it to pieces. It didn't have a squeaker inside, but I guess it looked like a dog toy. She really feels my deepest thoughts.

I'd hoped the Oklahoma trip would be boring, but they loved it + went sightseeing, including to the National Cowboy & Western Heritage Museum (which had the gift shop where they got the buffalo) + they took all kinds of pictures, including one where you put your face in a hole + there's a painted picture of a person's body below it. It makes them look like they are 2 cowboys swinging lariats. They both look so happy.

It's a TOTAL NIGHTMARE.

Now Javier's flying out for just 2 nights in the middle of next week because that's when he has a break from dancing + Dad is sending me to my friend Pippa's house for a sleepover! A SCHOOL NIGHT SLEEPOVER?!?!!? That's just plain wrong + maybe even against school rules. I could report him.

Dad took a duffel bag yesterday from the hall closet + started packing my stuff. You would think he was a pile-packer, which he is NOT. The Javier visit is NOT UNTIL A

WEEK FROM NOW! That's how excited he is. He can't wait to get me out of here.

When Dad was in my closet he found one of the CIGI T-shirts. He said, "We'll have to think about sending you to camp again this summer. Of course, CIGI will never let you in again, but there are lots of camps, so you can go someplace else." I was caught off guard, but I said, "I'd like to go to camp again, if Avery goes, too."

He looked sort of in pain + he said, "You CANNOT go to the same camp as Avery. First of all, she lives in New York. You need to find a place in California. Second of all, it's not a good idea."

What do you think? If we can't get THEM back together, maybe at least WE can find a way to see each other.

Do we both go to the same camp this summer + not tell them???

From: A. Allenberry Bloom
To: Bett Devlin
Subject: Camp

I told Papa, in a super-casual voice, that I was looking forward to camp this summer. I didn't say a word about going with *you*. I let him know that I'd like to pick the place myself, since he set up everything last year with CIGI, and doing research is my favourite way to relax.

But then later, when we were in the kitchen, he said,

"You wouldn't be thinking of going to camp with Bett Devlin – right? That wouldn't be a great idea."

Sometimes he's like a mind reader. I'm lucky that it's not very often.

I just stared at him and said, "Bett and I aren't friends."

He looked totally relieved, and he smiled as if a bag of rocks had been lifted off his back. But then I added, "We're more like sisters."

From: Bett Devlin
To: A. Allenberry Bloom
Subject: Re: Camp

Dad says that he's not sure now about camp because we've got a lot of expenses this year. These are all Javier's fault, but he didn't say that. I'm going to ask Gaga. She'll know what to do.

You + I agreed to tell the other person every little thing that happens, so here's something: Javier sent my dad a honey-baked ham yesterday! Who sends someone a ham? It's not even Easter yet + we're not near another ham holiday.

You don't eat meat, so you would REALLY NOT like this present.

Okay, the ham tasted pretty amazing. But still. Dad's at the market right now getting stuff to make split pea soup. He's never made split pea soup before. He's so out of control.

My darling baby girl, Betty II,

I'm sitting down in the doorman's little room in the lobby of the building on West 88th writing this. It's my day off. Since I can't pull weeds in my garden (which must have nothing BUT weeds in it now) I made walnut butterballs from my special recipe, and I'm sharing them with Dinos and Mateo (he's the FedEx man). He wears shorts no matter what the weather, and I like that about him.

I can only eat the walnut butterballs when I'm not working, because I feel allergic after a few of them and my tongue gets all thick! I'd be slurring my words onstage!

So the play's run got extended, did you hear? Those reviews really helped, especially that nice Jesse Green in the *New York Times*, who said I was "both old and young, and definitely an original".

I get stopped sometimes on the street now and people want to take a photo! I don't mind posing with folks. Why not? They get a little thrill, and so do I.

I saw Javier last week. I thought we were going to get to know each other (Hey, I speak Spanish, too), but instead, he was out on that little balcony for the longest time talking to your daddy on the phone.

I know you & Avery both want your dads to get back together but honey, I think you're going to have to let that go. It doesn't mean you girls can't be close.

Bett, I can explain life to you, but I can't understand

it for you. We've all got to get to that place ourselves. But I've got some extra money and I want to put it to good use. So here's what I've decided:

I'm going to pay for you to go to summer camp. Pick any place you want.

Follow your heart, darling. That's what I was writing to say. If you & Avery want to go to the same camp, that's fine by me. I'm not telling, and I mean that. I'm not great at keeping secrets, but you've got my word.

Love you forever,
Your Gaga

From: Bett Devlin
To: Betty Devlin
Subject: You're amazing, Gaga!

Thank you so much! I'm so so SO HAPPY!

I know camp costs a lot + even more if I leave the state. I told Dad about your offer to pay for it + he put his fist up into the air + pumped it + shouted: "YES!"

Anyone watching would have thought that HE was going to camp. I hope he's happy for me, not that he's just EXCITED TO GET ME OUT OF HERE for the summer.

I'm going to find a really good place. You + I won't be together like last summer, but you will be there with me on the inside (people always say "in spirit" but I think that's awkward to say to someone who's old because it sounds like they died + are now a ghost).

You're not OLD-OLD. I mean you're OLD, but not REALLY OLD. Plus you're in a Broadway play! That's the youngest thing ever.

Thanks again, Gaga.

Love you, which I already did before you agreed to pay for camp. I'm not going to write that I love you MORE now, because loving someone should never be connected to money or what they can do for you. That's a bad attitude.

Little Betty Devlin

From: A. Allenberry Bloom
To: Bett Devlin
Subject: Picking a camp

I sort of wish we could go back to CIGI, but we are banned for life, even though we were the victims of Camp Director Daniel's harsh judgment, which ended up being the greatest thing ever.

I'm making a spreadsheet of possible places for us to go. It's got categories that include the following:

Activities
Location

Size

Special focus

And whether they have a Parents' Weekend — we definitely don't want that!

From: Bett Devlin

To: A. Allenberry Bloom

Subject: Re: Picking a camp

Could you add in a category for caring for animals with hooves?

From: A. Allenberry Bloom

To: Bett Devlin

Subject: Re: re: Picking a camp

I just put in one for animals. I don't think we need to be specific about hooves. Kristina says I should go to a place with no rules. Are there summer camps with no rules? She also said it should be a place in the mountains, where you can yodel, or at least learn a new voice approach.

She sometimes has an unrealistic view of the world.

From: Marlow Devlin
To: Betty Devlin
Subject: Camp for Bett

Bett told me that you're paying her summer camp bill! I can't tell you how grateful I am. Last summer she talked about burning down the house if I sent her away. It's just great that she'll be able to have another chance at a camp experience. You've come to the rescue, Mom. Not just for Bett, but for both of us.

Javier and I are trying to take things slowly, but an opportunity came up. I'm going to come to NYC for the summer. Bett will be in camp (now I'm thinking the East Coast would be best), and Javier and I can see what it's like to be in the same city. I think I told you I just built a big fountain down in Riverside. The same company asked if I'd oversee a project for them in Brooklyn. It should take three to six months, and I've said I can do the first three. Dee is going to run the office and take care of the dogs. Thank God I didn't let Bett talk me into the miniature goats.

So I'll be getting paid. I'll be with Javier. And near you, of course. Who knows, maybe Sam and I can even figure out how to be friends. Or at least friendly. That's the report from here. But this is all just a big THANK YOU.

Love you, Ma.
Doug aka Marlow, but to you, always Doug

From: A. Allenberry Bloom
To: Bett Devlin
Subject: I've found the place!

Dogfish –

We talked about the farm camps (too many hooves for me) and the bike camps (we don't want to pound the pavement for miles, and that's too much exercise and sun exposure and also unsafe). Papa would probably pick a language-immersion camp, where they don't give you your cereal in the morning unless you conjugate a verb. Kristina's been pushing for the nonexistent, no-rules, arts-are-everything camp.

But here's what I think. If you study the spreadsheet I've attached, you'll see that the best match right now is a place called Camp Far View Tarn. It's for Girls Ages 7–15, in Bannister, Maine. It's basically the most traditional camp in the universe and it's been around forever.

The cabins look rustic. Everyone wears these green shirts and shorts. And the activities haven't changed in seventy-five years and they're proud of that. I find this attitude interesting, but it would also help our plan. They say there's no Wi-Fi. At first that sounded risky. But now I'm thinking that this means no pictures posted of us doing activities. Which means that we will be in no danger of our dads finding out we are together. There's so much to think about, living in a cyber world.

Hayley Bellinger went to a camp last summer where her parents could sit at home in front of their computers all day and watch the camp dining room and the boathouse in real time. Whenever they saw Hayley walking by the camera, they started screaming and jumping up and down and shouting her name as if she could hear them. Hayley's little brother, Owen, told Hayley that it was like she was a celebrity on a red carpet. That's so embarrassing.

If we pick Far View Tarn we will be in our own little cocoon away from the world, which is so filled with breaking news that it makes people (me) anxious.

What do you think? A very traditional summer camp could be right for us. After all, everyone tells us we don't live in "traditional" households even though my papa is about as conventional as they come. A lot of people don't realize a dad is a dad is a dad.

Should we give Far View Tarn a try?

From: Bett Devlin
To: A. Allenberry Bloom
Subject: Re: I've found the place!

I trust you, Avery. As long as you know they have horses + hiking trails I say yes.

I'll tell Dad (+ also Gaga) the news tonight. My dad is so distracted now with Javier + going East for the summer that he will probably just nod + say, "Let your Gaga know. She's sending the cheque."

I talked to Gaga about my dad + your dad + how sad we were that it didn't work out. She said I had to accept that my dad has someone new in his life + that kids can't make their parents do anything when it comes to "matters of the heart".

But what if Dad's relationship with Javier means I'll have to move to Cuba? At least I speak Spanish. I asked my dad + he said, "Oh, no, Javier would NEVER move back to Cuba, he's an exile."

So am I, now that they're playing online chess every night + talking for hours. But at least Far View Tarn means you + I will be together ALL SUMMER LONG.

B

2 MONTHS LATER

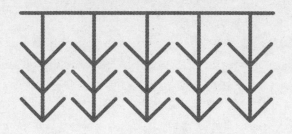

From: Bett Devlin
To: A. Allenberry Bloom
Subject: ON MY WAY

I am at the airport + I have a plastic badge around my neck that says Unaccompanied Minor. It's so limiting. There's a woman who's travelling with a service dog (named Tommy) + I already went to the counter + said I'd sit by Tommy if that would help out. Some people don't like to be next to animals while flying. I don't understand that.

Dad got me here early. It's the NEW DAD. He's now on time + he's growing his hair into a MAN BUN just like Javier. I like his hair short, but I told him it looked GREAT because he needs my support.

New T-shirt idea: LOVE MEANS NOTHING IN TENNIS. SO DOES HALF THE STUFF I SAY.

From: A. Allenberry Bloom
To: Bett Devlin
Subject: Re: ON MY WAY

I'm typing this on the bus. It actually wasn't that hard to get Papa to let me ride up to Maine by myself. Kristina kept saying that if Papa drove me, she would insist on joining us. So that helped.

Whenever I think of all the lies I've been telling about the summer, I feel guilty. But maybe it's not actual lying. It might be only giving partial information. The planning that goes into hiding something is extreme. Most criminals must be hard workers.

Pretty much all of the girls on this bus already know one another, because they've been "Tarnies" since they were seven years old. So no one sat next to me when we got on. They are now all jammed together in the back, which is unsafe because it unbalances the bus. They must have a lot of catching up to do.

It made me feel bad at first. Like I was a little kid and no one picked me for a dodgeball team. (Okay, obviously that's happened to me before. But there's nothing worse than dodgeball, so it wasn't tragic.)

I guess even at thirteen you're not too old to feel left out. But probably that's true at any age. Even when we're really old and in a nursing home there will probably be cliques.

Dear Parents,

I'm writing to let you know that all our campers have arrived safely and settled in well. Just a reminder that Far View Tarn believes our girls need to take a break from screens and give themselves over to nature, friendship, and character growth. The only communications you will receive from your daughters will be in handwritten form. Each girl is required to send at least two letters a week. We hope they send more! We provide stationery, and we check to make sure the envelopes are properly addressed and stamped.

I urge you to write back promptly to your girls, as they so look forward to receiving mail. But please, no care packages, and no photographs (including pets) that might make the campers homesick. We want to keep everyone focused on the Far View Tarn experience.

You have sent us your daughters, and we will return them to you at the end of the summer as fully formed "Tarnies".

Sincerely,
(Mrs.) Chessie Leonard, Camp Director

Dear Kristina & Papa (alphabetical order),

I'm writing you one letter. Papa, will you please scan it and email it to Kristina right away?

I made a big mistake coming here. I can live with the fact that my cabin has no electricity, and I can live with the very limited food options (which are not great for a vegetarian). But there's one thing I cannot live with.

The Tarn.

Do either of you even know what a "tarn" is? It's the word for "lake" in Scottish. The whole camp is focused on this huge body of water that's twenty or thirty miles across. And it's required that every camper row in a two-person canoe to the other side (which you can barely see) on the last week of camp. There are no exceptions.

I would never, ever have come here if I'd known about this. I've tried to explain to my counsellor, Jilly, that open (deep) water is a big problem for me, but she's not listening. Will you guys call and explain? Maybe also send a note from Dr Glossman? There isn't even a camp therapist, like at CIGI.

The only person paying attention to my situation is a very nice girl from somewhere out west. She's also a first-time Tarnie. All the others are in Year Five of Camp Cruelty.

I miss you guys so much. HELP!

Love,
Avery

Dear Papa & Kristina (reversing alphabetical order),

They won't let me call you. I tried. I'm writing again. For the first two days, I refused to get into the canoe. I pretended I had bad period cramps. But then Jilly said I had to row. And I honestly thought she might become violent. She said I was making her look bad and it would affect her end-of-summer report. I guess that's really important to her.

Before I got into the canoe I asked for earplugs, a nose clip, and the owner's manual for what I now know is called a Type II personal flotation device. It provides 15.5 pounds of buoyancy. I tried wearing two of them when I was in the canoe, so I would have 31 extra pounds of buoyancy, but I got way too hot and uncomfortable. (And anyway, the human body has on average a relative density of 0.98, which means that I'd float even without the devices. Supposedly.)

I really feel like I could still drown when I'm in the canoe. But obviously it would now be a lot harder.

Luckily I was able to be in the same canoe as the nice girl, and she doesn't care if I just pretend to paddle. Wearing the double flotation devices means it's hard to move my arms. I've kept my eyes shut for the first few rides and hummed as a distraction technique.

Please get me out of the long canoe trip. Or else please let me come home before it happens. I miss you guys so much. I don't think I can stay here.

Love,
Avery

Dear Dad,

YOU ARE NOT GOING TO BELIEVE THIS. We have NO ELECTRICITY in my cabin. NONE. There's NOT a power outage. THAT'S THE WAY THE CAMP RUNS.

We have lanterns at night (no candles because they think we'd burn down the place). I really didn't read much about Far View Tarn before I came here. I'm not complaining. I just want you to know that I feel LUCKY we have flush toilets.

It's all SUPER old-school. That's why you're getting a LETTER. Pen + paper (writing is required). It's like the Stone Age. Or the Paper Age. So I'm spending the summer in this really primitive place, except with a LOT of rules. Only they don't call them rules. They call them "traditions."

Jilly, our counselor, starts EVERY SENTENCE with, "One of our traditions here at Far View Tarn . . ." then she'll just straight up tell us to do something. Like, "One of our traditions here at Far View Tarn is to shower every night before bed, so get in there."

But Jilly's excited the way I'd be if you said, "One of our traditions here at Far View Tarn is to go on a roller coaster." Only obviously they don't have a roller coaster. That would require power. A girl named Annie November said that her brother, Rocco, is at a ROLLER COASTER CAMP. For real. They have a bus + the kids stay in motels + travel around to amazing amusement parks where kids ride each of the roller coasters 30 times. I'd REALLY like to trade places with that kid for a while.

So the BIGGEST camp tradition here is CANOEING EVERY DAY. Then in the last week of camp we all row to the other side of the lake, which is maybe 15 MILES across. We spend the night and row back the next day. That just seems like a lot of rowing to me.

But one girl in my cabin is AFRAID OF DROWNING, so I feel VERY bad for her. I guess she's from someplace without lakes. Someplace very, very dry. She might be from Dubai. She didn't know about the forced rowing when she signed up.

The kids here are all pretty nice, except for a snotty girl named BRIELLE, who I just stay away from. There aren't many people of colour + I'm the only one in my cabin who hasn't been to Europe. Can you believe that? They LOVE that the cabin only has lanterns. I guess if you grow up with a lot of privilege it feels like an adventure to not have a light switch.

Okay, I filled the pages so that's it for now. Write back. You're not supposed to send me anything like candy or chips OR beef jerky (the teriyaki kind). But if you were to put treats in a box + write on the outside: CONTENTS: BOOKS maybe they would get to me anyway. If you were super crafty, you could HOLLOW OUT A BOOK and drop something inside.

Love you, Daddy.
Bett

Dear Mom,

So far things are pretty good here at Far View Tarn. I liked the bus ride up because all the long time Tarnies sat together in the back and right away we started singing some of the songs and a lot of the older kids joined in, which is cool.

I got Jilly for my counsellor, which is not that great. I wish I had Ali H., but she's with the third-year kids this summer. She's better than Jilly. All of the girls from last year are back except for Mercer and Sill. I guess Mercer is at some other camp. No one knows about Sill.

We have two new girls in our cabin. I don't hang out with either of them. One is from New York and a total baby. She's afraid of the lake and doesn't want to canoe. I thought she'd go home but the other new girl is her friend and I guess she doesn't want to leave her or something. The other girl is from California. I really think that people from California act like they're cooler than people who aren't from there. I found out yesterday that BOTH of these girls have gay dads. That just makes no sense to me. Pretty weird, right?

Anyway, that's what's going on. Do you think when I get back I can get a new phone? Everyone here has been talking about stuff their phones can do and I'm just quiet. I'm glad that they can't see I'm two generations back with what I have.

Hope everything's okay at home.

Love,
Brielle

Avery –

I scanned and sent your letter to Kristina, and then I put in a call right away to the camp director, Mrs Leonard. She said that the situation is under control. Is that true? Your letter took four days to get here, so maybe I was reading old news.

Mrs Leonard said you were adjusting to the water activities and were now canoeing with your eyes open. She also said that the safety record at Far View Tarn is impeccable.

You'll get through this, sweetheart. And I'm guessing the summer will fly by. I hope you make some good friends. That nice girl in your cabin sounds great. I think you two should stick together.

I miss you tons, lovebug.

Love you –
Papa

My Avery,

I'm just so sorry. I can't believe a place that's supposed to be filled with outdoor fun is forcing a canoe trip. I called that person Mrs Leonard and she refused to put you on the phone. She said that the problem was solved, and that you were growing every day in new directions (she wouldn't get specific, so I don't know what that even means).

Should I believe her? She sounded confident (and pretty bossy), but that might just be her regular tone. It's hard to tell without looking at her body language. I called Sam to see if he thought we should take you out of camp. He didn't want to talk to me about it.

I feel paralyzed. The only thing I will tell you is that sometimes a person needs to confront her fears directly. Also, it sometimes helps to just open your mouth and release your vocal cords in a loud and long way. This vents anger and frustration. I have done it many, many times. Just ask my downstairs neighbours.

Avery, I'm thinking of you every second. I'm very thankful that there's a kind camper in your cabin.

Love you forever and ever,
Your Kristina

Dear Brielle,

Every day I walk to the mailbox, and every day I find nothing but bills and disappointing catalogs. Then today a letter from you arrived. Finally!

I'm not complaining. It's just that you know I wait for your letters because I miss you (and your brother) so much.

I heard from Tyler on Monday. Across the lake from you at Camp Stone Point on his second day some boy decided it was a good idea to throw a smoking marshmallow stick up in the air. Tyler was in the wrong place at the wrong time. So now he's got a blistered ear. It could have been a whole lot worse. I hope it doesn't show in the end-of-camp pictures.

I'm assuming you'll see him when the two camps get together for a dance. Let me know if his ear scabbed up okay. I'm not telling your father. If you write to him (you don't need to), do NOT bring it up. He made his choice when he left us not to know the details of your lives, and he tried to get out of sending you two to camp this summer, and this burned ear could give him more ammunition.

Sorry that Mercer and Sill didn't come back. They were good Tarnies. You wrote about the two new girls and said they both have gay dads. I am certainly the last person to care about how other people choose to live. But I'm wondering now about the sorts of kids who are coming to Far View Tarn these days. It used to be so different.

As for me, I'm trying to organize the guesthouse in the event that we have to sell and move. The lawyer said we'll fight your father to the end on that. But I don't want you to worry. This is your time to just have fun.

Love from
Your mother

Dear Dad (+ say hi to Javier, too),

How are you? I'm fine. It's letter-writing day here. No choice. Like pretty much everything around here. I've been very busy with canoeing, hiking + singing. It's not a theatre camp but they take the camp SONG stuff really really seriously.

I've made some cool friends but that one girl in my cabin named Brielle really thinks she's all that. She's got a best friend named Charlotte Canaday who does handstands + cartwheels about every 5 minutes. I do handstands + cartwheels but don't need to show everyone all the time.

The first day I got here Brielle saw the picture I brought of you + Phillip + I said you were my dads (I didn't explain about Phillip dying because it's not her business). Yesterday I was in the bathroom + I heard Brielle say to Charlotte, "Having a gay dad probably damaged her."

I flung open the door (I wasn't even finished going to the bathroom) + I said "WHAT?"

They were really embarrassed, but then they claimed they were talking about ANOTHER GIRL who was here last year + who has a gay dad. Really?! I could have made a big deal about it, but I decided to let it go.

I didn't feel like telling anyone this story. So I'm telling you. But don't worry. I'll deal with Brielle in my own way.

Love you, Dad.
Bett

P.S. WHAT DO YOU HEAR ABOUT JUNIE + RAISIN?
I'm not going to write that I miss them MORE THAN
ANYONE ELSE because that's not nice to say. How's Gaga?

Bett –

Loved getting a letter from you today. But hated the part
with the mean girls. I will contact the camp if you want me
to do that. Just let me know. I'm there for you. Always. You
don't have to fight all your own battles. That's what a dad
is for.

I'm working hard on the Brooklyn project. My biggest
hurdle is that I don't have my regular crew. But being here
gives me time with Javier. He's got horrible hours and his
performances are at night, so we're still struggling with
the schedule.

I've gone to see Gaga in three more performances. She
gets better every time.

Love you and miss you,
Your Dad

P.S. I'm working on the hollowed-out book idea. Expect
something soon.

My sweet girls,

I'm writing to you both and making a copy on the printer because I'd be saying a whole lot of the same thing if I did it twice. Plus I heard Avery already did a similar thing.

I never went to camp. I did go camping. I'd say those were the good old days but I never much cared for sleeping on hard dirt!

I heard from Kristina that Far View Tarn is big on canoeing. I'm so glad that Bett is there, but don't worry, I didn't let on that you two were together. Avery, I know you're afraid of deep water, but sometimes you've got to stick a toe into something icy.

The big news here in the city is we moved the play into the new theatre, which is much bigger and fancier. Kristina's really happy about that, but I miss the old place. A bunch of the people from our building went to see the show. Kristina got them all tickets & afterwards we got pizza. Dinos (the doorman) was with the group & it turns out he goes to the theatre and opera all the time! Everyone's got a surprise, that's for sure.

I've been busy, but I still manage to see your daddy & Javier. They seem to be getting along in a cozy way, and your daddy says Brooklyn's where it's all happening. I don't know what "it" is, exactly.

I hope you're following the rules, Bett. And Avery, I hope you're breaking a few. Love you two!

Your Gaga

Dear Papa & Kristina,

I don't want you to worry about me. I worry enough about me for all three of us. I guess I'd say that it's getting better here, and it is. But the lake is always out there staring me in the face.

I'm trying to speak up about things, and they are now serving tofu in the dining hall every night at the salad bar, so that's something.

We have a dance with the boys from Camp Stone Point on Saturday. It's one more thing to worry about, which might be good because I can't think about drowning in the lake at the same time as being anxious about standing around in awkward clumps with other Tarnies being bitten by mosquitoes. We never even met these boys but we're supposed to dance with them? It's a tradition. Everything here is.

That's my report. How's the city?

Your daughter,
Avery Allenberry Bloom

Dear Brielle,

I got a call from Chessie Leonard, and she said you and your brother got into a fight at the dance. I have to say I just can't believe you two manage to find a way to go at each other even when you're up in Maine at different camps where you're supposed to be having a good time.

I will not tolerate this. I take it that there was some name-calling. Chessie didn't go into specifics, but she said that she's having formal apologies written. Whatever that means.

Brielle, I can't handle one more thing. Straighten up and fly right. I completely regret marrying your father. Don't make me regret having kids.

Your mother

Hey, Avery,

It's Tyler from Stone Point Camp. I hope it's okay that I'm writing you. I want to explain what happened. We were doing this Truth or Dare thing before we left to go over to Far View Tarn, and I lost. So I had to be the first one to go ask somebody to dance.

You were standing by yourself but I guess waiting for

your friend to come out of the bathroom. I swear I didn't know who you were or anything about you. Everyone else was standing in little groups (except that one girl who kept doing the handstands).

When I asked you to dance and you said you didn't like the song, I thought that was a good answer because the music they were playing must have been from when they first opened the camp. Even the counsellors were laughing at how old it was.

Then I asked that girl with red hair who was tapping her foot to dance, so that I could get the Truth or Dare thing over with. Also, she said she knew how to jitterbug, whatever that is.

But then later, after someone finally figured out how to change the music, a lot of people were dancing, and when I came over it was because at that point I did want to ask you to dance.

I had no idea you were in my sister's cabin. When Brielle saw us (I think it was our third dance) and came up and said did I know I was with one of the two girls who had a gay dad, I didn't have any idea what she was talking about. That's when all the yelling started.

I feel bad that you might think I'm an idiot like my sister. I really don't care if your dad's gay. My dad lives in Florida now with his new girlfriend, Amber, who used to be a sales rep at our family's company, Mayhew Grease Collection Services. You probably don't know this, but all fast-food restaurants need their grease collected and taken away. It's super important for the environment. Anyway,

Amber's really nice but I would never tell my mom that.

I guess there's another dance coming up. I hope I see you there. Also, my friend Nick said that your friend (Bett? The one who got into the fight with my sister?) seemed really cool. Nick was the guy wearing the red hoodie, if your friend wants to know who he was.

Again, sorry that everything was so embarrassing.

Sincerely,
Tyler Mayhew

Hi, Tyler,

Thanks for writing to me. You didn't have to explain. I don't really hang out with your sister, even though we're in the same cabin.

My friend Bett says that your sister is jealous because our dads are pretty cool and my mom writes plays and Bett's grandma is acting in an Off-Broadway show. Bett's dad's boyfriend is a star of the Ballet Hispánico in New York City. We don't brag about any of that stuff, but it comes out. Just like we all know that Hannah Minter's parents own a casino in Matamoras, Pennsylvania (it's for sale right now). When you live with people, you get to hear the details of their lives.

I'll see you at the next dance if I'm still here. It's possible I'll be gone before then. There's a mandatory lake crossing in a canoe, and stuff might come up for me back in the city during that time, which would mean I'd have to leave early.

Sincerely,
Avery

Dear Gaga,

I like almost everyone in my cabin A LOT now, but that girl BRIELLE MAYHEW is a mess. She caused a fight at a dance we had with a boys' camp because me + Avery have gay dads. At least I think that's what started it. There was a lot of shoving + then the counsellors turned on the lights + started telling us to go to our cabins, and the boys had to get back on the bus.

How do you think my dad's doing with Javier? I'm okay if me + Dad end up packing up the church + moving to New York one day. I don't know what Junie + Raisin would think about snow on the sidewalks, but with you in New York + with Avery living there + Kristina, too, I can see how it would be okay for me. I would miss Angel + Summer + other friends + surfing. I'd miss all kinds of things, I guess.

One thing I know is that I'm not calling the shots. Maybe I never was. When I was little the slogan for Legoland down by San Diego was "Where Kids Call the Shots". I remember the first time Dad took me there I thought that I'd walk in + see kids running everything. They weren't. So the kids weren't really calling the shots. This was before the media literacy class at CIGI where they told us to look closely at all advertising.

Love you, Gaga. Thanks for always being there for me (nobody made me write that, but our counsellor, Jilly, just said, "Finish strong, girls!" (She runs track in college.)

xo
Bett(y) 2

Dear Papa & Kristina,

It's very up and down for me here. Good days and bad days. We had a second dance, and it was a lot better because nobody got in a fight. Plus we at least now know those boys. Or maybe we don't know them, but we've seen them before.

I'm obviously still worrying about the canoe trip. But they schedule a lot of things that aren't water activities. And they have us singing when we are on the move, so that takes up about five hours a day.

Sorry this letter isn't longer. Nobody checks anymore for length. They just collect the envelopes. I could send an empty one, but I wouldn't do that.

Love you and miss you.
Avery

Dear Angel –

I'm writing this from a hammock at Far View Tarn. I'm supposed to be telling you how cool it is here + also try to see if you want to come here next year. Okay. Did that. I'm having a good time. At first it wasn't that great, but now I've figured out the horse I really like (named Tri-Tip) + we play volleyball + also I like archery, soccer on the field + the rope-climbing stuff. Another thing that's pretty fun are these scavenger hunts. We divide into teams + we run around trying to find stuff. It can get intense. Also the food's really good + we sometimes make our own ice cream. It's really not that hard to do, but we have to turn a handle on this tub like we're in the olden times. I know there are automatic ice cream makers in the world where you just press a button, but electricity is a dirty word around here. I've got a bunch of new friends + they come from all over the place, but mostly from New York or Boston. Avery's doing okay. I came here because of her + we've had some fun, but she hates the lake + for some reason she gets more mosquito bites than anyone else in the world. She also has trouble going to sleep + she wakes up all the time in the middle of the night + I just can't be the person to talk to her at 3:00 a.m. I don't want to talk to ANYONE at 3:00 a.m. Anyway, I miss you. I'll be home in a few weeks. I'll tell you everything then.

I'll bring you a souvenir but it might just be a pinecone (very large).

Love,
Bett

Papa and Kristina –

I'm still spending a lot of my time with the girl from out west, but not as much as before because we don't do the same activities for a lot of the day. That's okay. I have permission to be alone sometimes in the mornings so I go back to the cabin and organize my stuff and try the meditation exercises that the nurse gave me. Jilly is okay with that as long as I stay on my bunk and don't wander off into the woods or go into the lake. I would never do either of those things and I think she knows that now.

I'm not going to say I'm counting the hours until summer is over because that's only part of every day. I have found some amazing flowers here that grow wild and are mostly very, very small and I've been pressing them in the books I brought. Most of the other campers never even see these tiny flowers. They don't even know that they're there.

Love you,
Avery

Gaga –

There was a second dance last week with the boys from that camp that's close by. I'm not going to say I have a boyfriend, because I DON'T. But I did dance a lot with one kid from Greenwich, Connecticut, named Nick, who smells like toast. In a good way.

Avery danced the WHOLE TIME with this kid Tyler who has a complicated background (maybe I told you he's the brother of Brielle).

I'm glad, because Tyler has given Avery something to talk about besides DROWNING. She's sort of driving me crazy about that. I think Tyler's relatives came over on the Mayflower (not the moving company. THE BOAT. Not kidding).

Love you, Gaga!
xxoo
Bett

Dear Dogfish,

It's late and everyone in the cabin is asleep, including you. I've got my emergency flashlight on.

It was a mistake to pick this place. The spreadsheets

didn't tell the full story. I'd say lesson learned, but I really don't know that I'll get out of here alive. I'm still so scared whenever we're in the canoe. It's a true fear vs some of my irrational ones, like being killed by a falling air-conditioning unit, though actually that happens more than you think.

But I might be awake right now because of something else.

I know I talk too much about the lake, and I feel like it's getting on your nerves. Are you mad at me, Bett? We don't always have to sit together, and everyone gets sick of each other at some point, so I'm thinking maybe that's why you left dinner early with Markie. Are you trying to get away from me? Do you want to do your own thing? It's okay if you do. I understand, I think.

I'm going to place this letter under your pillow (and hopefully not wake you up) and you can read it tomorrow.

xxx
Night Owl

Avery,

I got up to go to the bathroom + you're asleep now. But I just read your letter. I wasn't going to say anything, but you asked, so here's my answer. No, I'm not mad at you, only I really do wish you could GET OVER your stuff with canoeing. I also wish you'd stop asking so many questions about what's in the food (if they say there's no meat in it then just accept there's no meat) + also stop being kind of emotional about bug bites, night noises + bacteria on food.

We both have made other friends here this summer + we don't have to always be like partners in a three-legged race. By the way, I'd like to do that with Markie tomorrow. No offence, but I feel like she + I would win.

Maybe it's true that I'm trying to do things my own way sometimes. I mean, what do we really have in common? Once we had our dads, but that's over. I know you like Gaga, but she's MY GRANDMOTHER, not yours. I don't want to sound rude, but Avery I can't be there all the time to protect you from the world. It's sort of a full-time job.

I like when our cabin goes down to the lake to swim at night + I don't want to always stay back with you. I like riding the horses through the trees + not just on the path. I want to do a lot of the things you don't want to do.

I'm sorry. Avery, I really want to be friends, but I feel like you'll read this + take it all the wrong way. Only I still have to tell you the truth, because you asked.

Bett

B –

I put this in your cubby under your toothbrush because I want you to see it right away when you wake up.

I got up early and I asked Jilly to move me out of your canoe for the crossing. She said that was okay. You're going to be with Markie now.

You're right. We don't have that much in common. It's a good thing it didn't work out for our dads. It didn't work out for us, either, and probably for a lot of the same reasons. You and your dad are both reckless. And you don't realize it can hurt other people.

I'm going into town this morning with Mrs Leonard. I guess they're taking a girl from Poplar Cabin to see the doctor. She has an infected spider bite. I asked if I could go along to be supportive (only also because I want to see if they drain the lesion or give her a shot of antibiotics or both).

But don't worry, I won't bother you anymore.

Tomorrow we do the canoe trip and a week later we'll be gone from here.

AAB

Dear Kristina and Papa,

This is the last time I'll write you guys before the Big Dreaded Canoe Trip. It's tomorrow morning. We leave at 6:00 a.m.

I'm afraid. I know you've both said that fear gets a person nowhere, but that really hasn't been helpful advice. Sorry.

The counsellors say this trip is a bonding experience. How much more do we need to bond? We already eat, sleep, and do everything together. We've been here all summer.

At this point, I'm ready to unbond from these people, and I'm trying, believe me.

Anyway, you guys are right, it will be a blast.

Or not.

Okay, wish me luck.

Avery

From: Jilly Holland
To: Chessie Leonard
Subject: What happened today on the lake

You said I need to write to you and say exactly what happened, and that you want me to just state the facts. I'm really upset right now, but I'm going to try.

I'm twenty years old and a senior counsellor at Far View Tarn Camp in Maine. And though this is only my third year working here, I was a Tarnie myself for nine years, so I know everything at this camp really well. I have twelve campers in my group, which is Pinecone House.

Yesterday was the first day of the Tarn end-of-camp canoe trip, where we paddle across the lake, spend the night, and paddle home the next day.

The Tarn is eleven miles across and most of the canoes go about three miles an hour. It takes just under four hours to cross. The girls have been in training for this most of the summer, and all twelve of my girls were in good enough shape to do the crossing.

I have only one girl out of the twelve, Avery Bloom, who was nervous about making the trip.

Avery Bloom was in a canoe with Charlotte Canaday. Charlotte is my strongest oarer (she's a gymnast).

Brielle Mayhew was with Piper Tilley. And Bett Devlin was with Markie Bishop.

The rest of the girls had good matches (but that's not important to what happened).

Each canoe held the two campers, as well as our water kit, which has a signalling whistle, an emergency float throw line, and sponges. My canoe holds a larger first-aid kit. The girls take two water bottles apiece, plus four different healthy snacks.

The campers know that we follow the pace of the slowest canoe. We do not let one canoe get out ahead, and all canoes must remain within shouting distance. On the other side of the lake there are cabins outfitted for the night, so we didn't need to bring those supplies for the sleepover.

We made it across yesterday right on schedule. And we also spent the night without any problems. (Piper Tilley woke up at 3:00 a.m. and vomited – too many devilled eggs – but that didn't affect anything.)

Today we started back at 8:00 a.m. I was in a canoe with junior counsellor Sasha Pape. Our plan was to take three rest breaks. The bad thing happened during the last rest break, when we weren't far from shore.

I'm sorry, but I feel sick writing this, and I'm going to have to finish it later.

Is there any update about the girls? I wanted to go in the ambulance but they wouldn't let me.

I'm so sorry, Mrs Leonard. I don't know what else to say. I'm just so sorry.

From: Sunny Mayhew
To: James Mayhew
Subject: There was an accident today at Far View Tarn

Jim –

Brielle is okay, but she's in the hospital up in Maine. So are two other girls. I'm driving up there right now. You could get a plane from Newark. I'll be on my mobile, so call me. I just left you a message. It's ridiculous that we haven't been talking. That's over, Jim. Call me.

Sunny

From: Sasha Pape
To: Mrs Chessie Leonard
Subject: Accident today

I want to say right up front that we didn't know a lot about what happened because four of the seven canoes were at a distance from the ones where the accident took place. All of the canoes were taking a ten-minute rest break. But our four canoes were singing (a round in three-part harmony) at a distance. (The wind had come up and we were drifting and it was blowing us west.) Because of the singing and also because we weren't close, we didn't know there was a problem until the emergency whistle started blowing and by then the girls were already in the water.

So this is what Jilly and I were both told (not what we saw). Markie Bishop was in the front of her canoe with Bett Devlin in the rear. The girls were horsing around (we were almost finished with the eleven-mile crossing). Markie, holding her paddle, tried to stand up in her canoe. (She does have great balance, but standing up is absolutely not allowed.) Markie lost her balance and started to fall. When this happened she let go of her paddle. It then struck

Bett Devlin on the temple and she fell over, with her head hitting the metal edge of the right side of the canoe.

The other girls saw Bett's hand go up and there was blood but then a second later she slumped over (I guess knocked out) and she fell right into the water.

But Bett wasn't wearing her life jacket. She had taken it off a few minutes earlier because it was so hot out, even though this is against the rules. (Obviously Jilly and I didn't see her take it off.) Charlotte Canaday and Markie Bishop had also taken off their life jackets. We didn't see that, either.

Bett Devlin was now facedown in the water. The next thing to happen was that Avery Bloom dove out of her canoe, which then tipped over, sending Charlotte into the water. (Charlotte had no life jacket on, but she's a strong swimmer.)

Avery (wearing her life jacket) swam to Bett and was able to flip her over. I guess there was blood in the water. Piper Tilley (in her canoe with Brielle Mayhew) then fainted. (She was the one who had vomited the night before.)

Avery took off her life jacket and positioned it under Bett to keep her head up. But that was a real struggle and Avery (not a great swimmer) started to swallow water. She now didn't have on a flotation device and she then went under. It's possible at this point she had a panic attack because Charlotte said it was like Avery suddenly couldn't breathe.

Brielle then dove in and swam to Avery.

This is when we heard the emergency whistle.

Charlotte (still in the water) reached over Piper and got the emergency kit.

Once we got over there and realized what was going on, Jilly took her mobile and called 911.

I think you heard the rest.

From: Marlow Devlin
To: Sam Bloom
Subject: The HOSPITAL is at 1800 Emerald Bay Road

AVERY WILL BE OKAY, Sam. That's the most important thing for you to know. She was breathing on her own when they got her back in the canoe. I tried to call and text you again, but it didn't go through. I think you're still in the air. I was lucky to get that first flight. I CANNOT believe the girls were together at camp this whole time. How did we not KNOW that? I flew to Portland and drove a rental car here, going about a hundred miles an hour, but somehow I didn't get pulled over. I think your voicemail said you were flying into Bangor. I'm in Bett's room right now. She's sedated because of the head injury. They've got a neurologist in here.

I need Bett to be okay. She's my kid, my girl.

Sam, she's my whole life.

Voicemail: From Kristina Allenberry

Avery, you are the bravest person I've ever known. I've been scared of many things in my life. Failure. Success. Being responsible for a baby. You jumped into the water and instantly overcame fear to save a life.

Your dad and I feel like such fools. We didn't know you and Bett were both at camp together. But thank goodness you were.

At the theatre we all just joined hands and closed our eyes, and though I'm not a religious person in the traditional sense, Gaga led us in a prayer for you and Bett. We said aloud: Dear God, or Dear Whoever, be there for these girls. Please, be there.

Darling, we are on our way up there now. Me. Gaga. Dinos from the building is driving us. We are on our way. We will see you soon and all of this will be said in person.

I'm so proud to be your mother. Always. And forever.

From: Betty Devlin
To: Bett Devlin
Subject: My darling baby girls

Bett & Avery –

I'm writing this for me as much as for you two. I'm admitting that. I can't sleep. Putting words down feels like I'm

269

talking to you girls. I need to talk to you. I'll always need that.

I know you're both going to be all right. You're my little girls, the ones I never got to have, what with only one son and then a husband who died young. Bett, and then you, Avery, have filled all the holes in my life. I didn't know they were even there until you came along.

The main nurse at the hospital told us all to leave. The only person they let stay was Doug. He's allowed to sleep in the chair next to you, Bett. I'm guessing the rest of us were causing too much of a racket. Sam wanted to sleep in your room, Avery, but they said no. You're in stable condition and there's another patient in your hospital room and I guess they thought it was too much.

Dinos the doorman drove me & Kristina up here. It took us almost nine hours. He's got a new Prius, which gets great gas mileage. When we got to the hospital we ran in & saw Doug & Sam just holding on to each other. Like they were in a storm & it was knocking them both over. They were crying & then we all started crying. Even Dinos, who barely knows you girls.

You're not out of danger yet. Sometimes these things take a while. So we'll just let you take your time.

Avery, you were a hero today. And so was that girl Brielle. I know you had trouble with her, but it seems she pulled you both out. They brought her to the hospital, too. For "observation". They said she went into shock once you got onshore. Life's one big mystery, that much I know.

So right now we're at the motel. They only had one room left because August is the busiest time. Dinos is on a cot.

Sam's on the bed sleeping next to Kristina. She's got an arm flung around him. I took a picture, because I don't want them to ever forget. I'm on the pullout couch. I know I'm not going to sleep, so why give any of them this mattress with the lumps? We're going right back to the hospital first thing in the morning.

My understudy went on at the theatre & the report back was that she was really great. That got me thinking that I want to go home to Texas for a while. I'll come back in a bit, but I need to see my little cat, Cinnamon, and my overgrown garden. I want to drive around town and swat flies on the back porch & complain about the heat to my friend Diamond. I want to try and "binge-watch" whatever everyone says is good on TV that I've been missing.

But what I really want is for my baby girls, Bett and Avery, to be okay.

That's all I need in the world.

I want yesterday back.

Love,
Your Gaga

From: Marlow Devlin
To: Javier Martinez, Sam Bloom, Kristina Allenberry, Betty Devlin, Dinos Tombras
Subject: THE GIRLS!

I couldn't sleep much in the chair so I got up and went down to the second floor for a cup of coffee. When I got back to the room I had the shock of my life. Bett wasn't in her bed.

I freaked and ran into the hall (spilling the coffee – anyone who brought another shirt, could you bring it over for me?). A nurse said that Bett was fine. But then we both went looking for her. Bett, pulling her IV stand, had somehow found her way to Avery's room. And she'd climbed up into the bed alongside Avery.

And that's where they were when I came into the room. Bett and Avery, both fast asleep in room 304. Doing fine. Doing more than fine.

From: Sam Bloom
To: Marlow Devlin
Subject: Going back to the city

Marlow –

Please assure me you were telling the truth when you said it was okay for Avery and me to leave and go back to the city this afternoon.

We would've stayed in Maine as long as you needed, and I hope you know that. Marlow, life is so precious. I know that's obvious, but it was all I could think the whole time at the hospital.

I'll call you tonight when we get home. If there's anything you need, well, you know the rest of that sentence.

Sam

From: Jilly Holland
To: Sam Bloom
Cc: Marlow Devlin
Subject: The accident on the lake

Hi, Mr Bloom and Mr Devlin,

It's Bett and Avery's counsellor, Jilly, here. We met in the hallway of the hospital by the vending machines. You may not remember, because I know you were pretty freaked out.

We're so relieved that the girls are both going to be okay!!!

I am writing today with a poem from the other campers of Pinecone House. The girls were really shaken up after what happened. Some of them went home early. We decided that those who stayed could write something. I think poetry makes everything a little bit better. We had a talent contest, so Pinecone House set this to music (we tried to do it to "The House of the Rising Sun", but it didn't really sound like it). We came in third.

Sincerely,
Jilly Holland

The Ballad of a Scary Canoe Trip

The Far View girls went out in a canoe.
The morning was bright with sun and with dew.
The day was fair and all was well
Till an incident on the water turned heaven into hell.
A girl made an error, and an oar it did slip.
It happened so fast, and a canoe side Bett did hit.
But Avery showed bravery, and Brielle did, too.
They are both superheroes, and Tarnies through and through.

We love our dear Bett, and are glad that Fate missed her,
And we also love Avery, who we think of as Bett's sister.

The summer here is a long one, without electricity to guide us,
But in darkness and in light, we always have our friends beside us.

Love,
Everyone in Pinecone House

From: Avery Bloom
To: Bett Devlin
Subject: Going home

Bett, I don't know when you'll read this since they told us you have to be off everything electronic for a while because of the concussion, but Papa and I came down the hall to say good-bye. The door to your room was closed and they said you were getting a sponge bath and it was going to take a while. That sounds so awkward. And also, is it sanitary? Okay, stopping that train of thought.

I know you said not to say again that I'm sorry I got super-annoying at camp, only I have to because I have to overdo everything. It's the nature of all owls (just made that up). You said you were sorry, too, for being insensitive and always wanting to do things your way.

But I think it's not bad to have a blowup with someone you really care about. Once that happens, you can be even closer. Maybe because sharing bad things as well as good things means you're in it for real. That's what being honest with someone does.

I feel that way about what happened with us. And not just because after our fight we both almost died in that incredible health hazard that is called a tarn. But also because 1) I care about you, and 2) you make me feel good about who I am.

We both know we are now lifetime Tarnies! I'm never going back there, but that doesn't mean I won't think about that place every day for the rest of my life. And here's a really good and shocking thing that happened while you were in bad shape and I was recovering from taking a gallon of lake water into my lungs:

The dads are no longer enemies. It took our near-death experiences for them to finally have their reconnecting moment. So far I haven't even been yelled at for going to the same camp as you but not telling Papa and Kristina. Maybe that will come later.

The nurse told us you need to stay in the hospital until the neurologist says you can go. I wish I could be there for those tests, for all kinds of reasons. Neurology is considered the most difficult of all the medical specialties.

I was so afraid about the canoe trip, and I was right that it would be a problem. But I'm thinking real problems are the ones you can't see coming. Maybe that's why they're real problems. On the plus side, I've got an awesome college essay topic: "How I Sort of Saved a Life at Summer Camp, With Help from an Unlikely Fellow Camper".

But not just "a" life. The life of my best friend. My sister (by choice). My dogfish.

xo

P.S. They packed up all our stuff for us and brought it over to the hospital. Hey, news flash! Tyler was going home with Brielle but he left me his green Stone Point Camp hoodie with a note that said maybe he and Brielle would meet me sometime in the city. It could happen. Also, I met the parents.

From: Bett Devlin
To: Avery Bloom
Subject: Bravery + Avery

Night Owl –

I FINALLY got a laptop in here. This concussion stuff
is really boring. It's just a lot of sleeping. No phone. No
TV. Nothing electronic. Until just now! I get 10 minutes
to write you. They are worried about overstimulating
my brain. Or something like that. So here we go: One
second I'm sitting in a canoe + the next I'm whacked in
the head by Markie Bishop + now here I am in a hospital
on Day 5.

Night Owl, I agree with EVERYTHING you said. I keep
thinking about what would have happened if YOU hadn't
been in the next canoe. Would someone else have jumped
in in time? I'll never know.

But I do know I'm always going to wear my life jacket
when I'm boating + I'm never going in another canoe with
Markie Bishop. (Although her parents DID send me a box
of really fancy sea-salt CARAMELS on Day 3. But I think
it's so we don't sue them.)

I heard that one of the cooks shot video on her phone
when they took us away. If it's true, I want to see it.
Especially if we're both being loaded into the back of the
same ambulance. I bet that won't be something that goes

into next year's Camp Far View Tarn's video of A Look at Our Tarnies!

Love you, Night Owl.
Dogfish

P.S. It's cool that Tyler and Brielle might come see you in New York!

From: Avery Bloom
To: Bett Devlin
Subject: Checking in

Gaga took a picture of Kristina and Papa asleep on the bed at the motel up in Maine. She's got her arm around him. She sent it to me, and I printed it out on Tuesday and framed it. Whenever my Papa sees it he laughs.

Did you know our dads have been speaking on the phone all the time since you guys left the city and flew back to LA? Isn't that amazing?

Do we get credit for all of this? My dad takes the phone into his study when he's talking, where I can't hear him. Can you read their email? Can we find out what's going on with them?

I'll call you later today. I'm going to see my mom and I'll

also see Gaga. It's weird that I just typed mom instead of Kristina. Wow.

Love from
Night Owl

From: Bett Devlin
To: Avery Bloom
Subject: NEWS

My dad finally stopped writing his email password on an envelope in his sock drawer. He's lost to me now. Or at least reading all his stuff is lost. I can still get into the Expedia account (he didn't change that password).

GUESS WHAT! I saw that there are tickets to go to New York. I'm not going to say anything. Standing by for life-changing news.

THREE MONTHS LATER

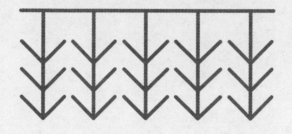

From: Avery Bloom
To: Bett Devlin
Subject: Important question

WHAT ARE YOU GOING TO WEAR?

WE HAVE TO COORDINATE. WE SHOULD NOT WEAR THE SAME THING, BUT ON THE OTHER HAND WE SHOULD WEAR SOMETHING THAT COMPLEMENTS EACH OTHER. THAT SPELLING IS DIFFERENT FROM COMPLIMENTS BECAUSE OF COURSE COMPLEMENTS WITH AN E MEANS "GOES WELL TOGETHER". WORDS ARE SO REASSURING TO ME. I'M CONSTANTLY TESTING MYSELF TO SEE IF I SUFFERED VOCABULARY DAMAGE FROM LACK OF OXYGEN WHEN I WAS UNDERWATER. SO FAR SO GOOOOOOD. HA!

ANYWAY, THIS IS SO EXCITING! JUST BEYOND EXCITING! IT'S SOMETHING ELSE. CAN'T THINK OF THE WORD, BUT THAT DOESN'T MEAN ANYTHING.

FORGIVE THE CAPS. MAYBE I AM YELLING. I FEEL LIKE IT!

DON'T SAY YOU SAW THIS COMING (AND SO FAST!) BECAUSE I DON'T BELIEVE YOU!

From: Betty Devlin
To: Bett Devlin, Avery Bloom
Subject: Things I want to say

Girls –

I've got a few things I want to put in writing before the big day. I'm starting with the headline. I love you.

That sentence just can't be worn out. I'm hoping when I take my last breath on earth, those are my last words. And fingers crossed that's not for a long, long time, but you never know.

With the wedding coming, I've been thinking about what it means to raise a child. The two of you are as bright as new pennies, and there's a whole lot of stuff you should be telling me. But this is my letter, so right now this is my turn.

Alden Devlin left this world too soon, but he did his job. He wasn't perfect, and he struggled to understand his boy. But it got easier over time. He learned acceptance – they both did. Alden showed Doug (or Marlow – why he went and changed his name is just nothing but irritating) how to be a parent. That's what this living thing is all about. There's a lot of teaching. But it's best by example. A good parent gets his child ready to take on his own child.

Bett, your daddy's been brave. He had courage about loving from an early age. And the teaching goes both ways. The child shows the parent as much as the parent shows the child.

So your daddy taught me to be brave in life because I saw that he could be. That's the circle. Doug (okay, okay, Marlow) met Sam in Chicago & they were both single men raising daughters. They both loved their little girls. These men wanted you two to be friends, and they were hoping (one day) sisters.

You're sisters now. You faced the tests & came out the other side.

A family's always changing shape. That's what I wanted to say before the wedding. In the last year, ours has just gotten bigger and better.

I love you both. And I always will.

Your Gaga

From: Avery Bloom
To: Bett Devlin
Subject: Rehearsal Dinner

Dogfish –

Tonight was really fun. I love staying up so late. Right now I'm looking at the moon, which is apparently a waxing gibbous. That's an ugly name, but the moon's beautiful.

Or maybe everything looks beautiful on the night before a wedding.

THE MORNING
AFTER THE WEDDING

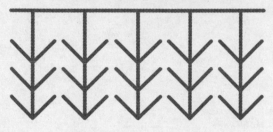

From: Bett Devlin
To: Betty Devlin
Cc: Avery Bloom
Subject: A toast! A toast!

Gaga,

This is from both of us. But I'm typing. We shouldn't be awake, especially since we danced until 2:00 a.m. But neither of us could sleep after the sun poked through the blinds. We're still too excited.

So, since we're already up, we're doing what you asked last night + sending you our wedding toast.

It might not read as well as when we said it. Maybe it's like pictures. It's better to look BAD in them but GOOD in real life than the other way around. Only maybe in the digital world it's better to look GOOD in pictures + BAD in real life because the pictures are shared + establish your brand.

We worked on the toast separately. Then went back + forth, just like you're supposed to do with group projects in school – only this was for real. (In school there's always one person in those things who does nothing.)

We weren't expecting you to cry. We figured our dads would cry. They do that pretty easily.

Avery just said even the bartender cried, but she thinks

it was seasonal allergies. Or how many limes he had to squeeze.

When you saw us give this speech we switched parts every time there was a double line space. We don't think it matters when you read it on paper.

A TOAST

Tonight we are here to celebrate a wedding.

This is the first real wedding for both of us. We can't believe this is happening. We love you so, so much + it's a dream come true to have an actual wedding in our own family.

We know about weddings mostly because you can't ever go to a haircut place without seeing a whole magazine called *BRIDES*. We've never seen one that says GROOMS, which is another example of discrimination. We will always be on the lookout for that in life.

We're both 13 now + compared to much older people we haven't experienced a lot of things, but here's what we have seen:

The way one story ends, but then starts up again.

The way families are made from people who want to be together more than they want to be apart.

The way no one can tell you what is or isn't a family. Well, they can tell you, but you don't have to listen and you shouldn't listen. You need to only listen to your heart.

The way worrying is sometimes about the wrong thing.

The way some people are bold + some people are more scared, but once in a while the parts SWITCH.

The way you can discover love when you don't expect it – a love for a person, or even for a new job, like suddenly becoming an actress, when you never did anything like that before.

The way people who are really different from each other can come together and their lives can merge, even if once in a while they get on each other's nerves, which is just a human thing.

The way some people are meant to be together.

The way some people aren't meant to be together.

At first, we thought our dads weren't supposed to be a couple.

But then we got to know each other + it felt like the greatest thing to happen to them.

Because we realized it was the greatest thing for both of us.

We wanted to be sisters. We would be Bett + Avery Devlin-Bloom, which is better than Bett + Avery Bloom-Devlin, rhythmically.

Only the more we got excited for this to happen, the more it all fell apart for our dads + we couldn't stop that.

No one's supposed to tell anyone, "You two shouldn't love each other." But maybe, also, no one's supposed to tell anyone, "You two *should* love each other."

What we wanted was a bigger family. We wanted a celebration. We wanted a wedding. Tonight, we got that.

It's not because of us. But we helped. We are Night Owl + Dogfish. One of us is wise like an owl + stays up late observing things. And the other one is fierce like a shark + is always on the move. Maybe it seems like we have nothing in common, but that isn't true. Together, we cover land + sky + sea. Together, we are a team.

But this, right now, is about another team. It's about how Dinos + Gaga – some people call her Betty – fell in love.

They aren't the same age. (Sorry, Gaga, but it's just a fact that you've got a few years on Dinos.) They don't come from the same place. Or have the same background. But Gaga lost her husband, Alden. And Dinos lost his wife, Calista.

Gaga is an actress now living in New York and Dinos is the main doorman in her building. Gaga is from Texas. Dinos is from Greece.

And they love each other.

They discovered this in his Prius, driving up to Maine.

It wasn't just Gaga's ability to figure out directions when the Google Maps app stopped working.

Or that Dinos needed new dental work after he ate Gaga's homemade peanut brittle, but still asked for more of it.

It wasn't only that Dinos makes the best coffee in the world, and loves opera + theatre + sardine sandwiches.

It was something bigger that they see in each other that makes them both want to hold on + not let go.

They animate each other's souls.

That's why we're here tonight.

Gaga and Dinos, you're just starting out in your new life. We – Avery Allenberry Bloom and Bett Garcia Devlin – want to say that we will always be there for you.

All of the people in this room are here to say the same thing.

Families can look different now from how they used to. And sisters can look different, too.

Gaga and Dinos: YOU are our grandma and grandpa. In all the ways that count.

And Dad and Papa, you're now friends.

We think you always will be. You shared a wild motorcycle ride across China. Because of that, Kristina is a big part of our lives today.

And when that happened, Gaga and Dinos came together.

So many friends from so many places are here. People from Greece. People from Texas. Judge Evan, who married you. Actors + the crew from the play *HOLDING UP HALF THE SKY*. Even some of our fellow campers from two different summers at two different camps. (Shout out to Brielle + Tyler + Piper + Dilshad +

Jasmine!) Members of the doorman's union Local 32BJ
+ and, of course, all the relatives.

We were very excited to meet Dinos's three kids, Helen,
Vivi, and Demetri and their families. Epolia, you're Dinos's
granddaughter and now Gaga's new granddaughter, and
you're exactly our age! What do you think about summer
camp?

Jalen + Billy, you just got 2 new babysitters. We can't
wait to spend more time with you.

There's going to be a special dance after you all drink
the champagne.

Dinos + Gaga will start. Then Gaga's going to dance with
Marlow. Then Dinos takes Vivi, and then he takes Helen.
From there, Avery's coming on to the floor with Sam. I've
got my dad. Vivi switches to Coco. Silvia + Syd join in.

Kristina will hit the dance floor with Daniel Birnbaum
from Camp CIGI. (It's a surprise to us that you two stayed
in touch, but not a problem.)

After that, we want all of YOU out there.

Here is the last thing: Everyone should just try to move
like Javier.

We won't look the same, but he knows his stuff.

Dancing is a way of setting your spirit free. We didn't come up with that – Javier told us.

Here's to families. To dads, moms, brothers + sisters + grandparents + uncles + aunts + cousins.

HERE'S TO LOVE.

HERE'S TO US ALL.

ACKNOWLEDGEMENTS

We would like to thank our two editors, Lauri Hornik + Julie Strauss-Gabel, who are also our two publishers at Dial and Dutton.

We want to acknowledge our gratitude to the president of Penguin Young Readers, Jen Loja.

We need to express our gratitude to the publicity, promotion, education, and sales teams at PYR.

We have to say that our agents are everything to us – Thank you, Amy Berkower, Suzanne Gluck, Anna DeRoy, and Cecilia de la Campo.

HOLLY GOLDBERG SLOAN

(hollygoldbergsloan.com) is the author of five previous novels for children and young adults, including the *New York Times* bestsellers *Short and Counting by 7s* (an E.B. White Read Aloud Honor Book). A graduate of Wellesley College who has written feature films such as *Angels in the Outfield*, Holly lives in Santa Monica, California.

MEG WOLITZER

(megwolitzer.com) is the *New York Times* bestselling author of *The Female Persuasion*, *The Interestings*, and *The Wife*, among other novels for adults; the young adult novel *Belzhar*; and the middle-grade novel *The Fingertips of Duncan Dorfman*. She lives in New York City.